STRESSED OUT

KEEPING YOUR COOL

		ENTRY LEVEL	ADVANCED LEVEL
SESSION 1	**Getting Acquainted**	Too Busy Luke 10:38–42	
SESSION 2	**Stress From Worry**	Worry Warts Matthew 6:25–34	Winning Over Worry James 1:2–11
SESSION 3	**Stress From Work**	Stress in the Workplace Matthew 20:1–16	The Workaholic 2 Cor.11:16–33
SESSION 4	**Stress From Failure**	Career Crisis Luke 22:54–62	Fail-Safe Romans 7:7–25
SESSION 5	**Stress From Conflict**	Conflict Resolution Mark 11:15–19	Loving Relationships Romans 12:9–21
SESSION 6	**Stress From Loss**	Lost and Found Luke 24:13–35	Ultimate Hope Romans 8:18–25,31–39
SESSION 7	**Stress From Overload**	Wear and Tear Matthew 26:36–46	Beating Overload 2 Cor. 1:3–11

Serendipity House / P.O. Box 1012 / Littleton, CO 80160

TOLL FREE 1-800-525-9563 / www.serendipityhouse.com

98 99 00 01 / **101 series • CHG** / 4 3 2 1

PROJECT ENGINEER:
Lyman Coleman

WRITING TEAM:
Richard Peace, Lyman Coleman, Andrew Sloan, Cathy Tardif

PRODUCTION TEAM:
Christopher Werner, Sharon Penington, Erika Tiepel

COVER PHOTO:
© Karen Su / FPG International LLC.

CORE VALUES

Community:	The purpose of this curriculum is to build community within the body of believers around Jesus Christ.
Group Process:	To build community, the curriculum must be designed to take a group through a step-by-step process of sharing your story with one another.
Interactive Bible Study:	To share your "story," the approach to Scripture in the curriculum needs to be open-ended and right brain—to "level the playing field" and encourage everyone to share.
Developmental Stages:	To provide a healthy program in the life cycle of a group, the curriculum needs to offer courses on three levels of commitment: (1) Beginner Stage—low-level entry, high structure, to level the playing field; (2) Growth Stage—deeper Bible study, flexible structure, to encourage group accountability; (3) Discipleship Stage—in-depth Bible study, open structure, to move the group into high gear.
Target Audiences:	To build community throughout the culture of the church, the curriculum needs to be flexible, adaptable and transferable into the structure of the average church.

ACKNOWLEDGMENTS

To Zondervan Bible Publishers
for permission to use
the NIV text,
The Holy Bible, New International Bible Society.
© 1973, 1978, 1984 by International Bible Society.
Used by permission of Zondervan Bible Publishers.

Questions and Answers

PURPOSE

1. What is the purpose of this group?

In a nutshell, the purpose is to get acquainted and to double the size of the group.

STAGE

2. What stage in the life cycle of a small group is this course designed for?

This 101 course is designed for the first stage in the three-stage life cycle of a small group. (See diagram below.) For a full explanation of the three-stage life cycle, see the center section.

GOALS

3. What is the purpose of stage one in the life cycle?

The focus in this first stage is primarily on Group Building.

GROUP BUILDING

4. How does this course develop Group Building?

Take a look at the illustration of the baseball diamond on page M5 in the center section. In the process of using this course, you will go around the four bases.

BIBLE STUDY

5. What is the approach to Bible Study in this course?

As shown on page M4 of the center section, there are two tracks in this book. Track 1 is the light option, based on stories in the Bible. Track 2 is the heavier option, based on teaching passages in the Bible.

THREE-STAGE
LIFE CYCLE
OF A GROUP

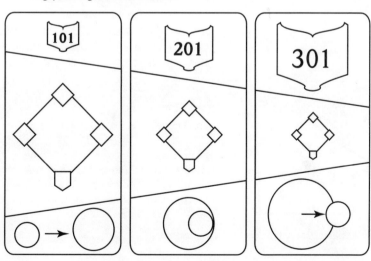

3

6. Which option of Bible Study is best for our group?

Track 1 is the best option for people not familiar with the Bible, as well as for groups who are not familiar with each other. Track 2 is the best option for groups who are familiar with the Bible *and* with one another. (However, whenever you have new people come to a meeting, we recommend you switch to Track 1 for that Bible Study.)

7. Can we choose both options?

Yes, depending upon your time schedule. Here's how to decide:

STUDY	APPROXIMATE COMPLETION TIME
Story Sharing only	60–90 minutes
Epistle Study only	60–90 minutes
Story and Epistle Study	90–120 minutes

8. What if we want to do both the Story and Epistle Studies but don't have time at the session?

You can spend two weeks on a unit—the Story Questionnaire the first week and the Epistle Study the next. Session 1 has only one Bible Study—so you would end up with 13 weeks if you followed this plan.

9. What if you don't know anything about the Bible?

No problem. The Story option is based on a parable or story that stands on its own—to discuss as though you are hearing it for the first time. The Epistle Study comes with complete reference notes—to help you understand the context of the Bible passage and any difficult words that need to be defined.

THE FEARLESS FOURSOME!

If you have more than seven people at a meeting, Serendipity recommends you divide into groups of 4 for the Bible Study. Count off around the group: "one, two, one, two, etc."—and have the "ones" move quickly to another room for the Bible Study. Ask one person to be the leader and follow the directions for the Bible Study time. After 30 minutes, the Group Leader will call "Time" and ask all groups to come together for the Caring Time.

10. What is the mission of a 101 group?

Turn to page M5 of the center section. This course is designed for groups in the Birth stage—which means that your mission is to increase the size of the group by filling the "empty chair."

11. How do we fill the empty chair?

Pull up an empty chair during the group's prayer time and ask God to bring a new person to the group to fill it.

12. *What is a group covenant?*

A group covenant is a "contract" that spells out your expectations and the ground rules for your group. It's very important that your group discuss these issues—preferably as part of the first session.

13. What are the ground rules for the group? (Check those that you agree upon.)

❐ PRIORITY: While you are in the course, you give the group meetings priority.

❐ PARTICIPATION: Everyone participates and no one dominates.

❐ RESPECT: Everyone is given the right to their own opinion and all questions are encouraged and respected.

❐ CONFIDENTIALITY: Anything that is said in the meeting is never repeated outside the meeting.

❐ EMPTY CHAIR: The group stays open to new people at every meeting.

❐ SUPPORT: Permission is given to call upon each other in time of need—even in the middle of the night.

❐ ADVICE GIVING: Unsolicited advice is not allowed.

❐ MISSION: We agree to do everything in our power to start a new group as our mission (see center section).

Getting Acquainted

3-PART AGENDA

ICE-BREAKER
15 Minutes

BIBLE STUDY
30 Minutes

CARING TIME
15–45 Minutes

While at times most of us have felt worn out and run-down, some of us experience the more serious effects of chronic stress and burnout—that state of physical, emotional and spiritual exhaustion. Chronic stress and burnout come on as slow fizzles and not explosions. And many of us are not aware of these problems until we smell our psychological and spiritual wires burning.

Some of the most common physical symptoms are fatigue and exhaustion, insomnia and nagging physical ailments, such as frequent stomach upset, headaches, muscular aches, etc. In addition, chest pains, heart palpitations, and high blood pressure are common. Some of the most common emotional and spiritual symptoms include irritability, anxiety, depression, excessive anger, disillusionment, cynicism and bitterness.

In the following studies, we will look at some of the common causes of excessive stress and examine what the Bible has to say about them. More specifically, we will look at worry, work, failure, conflict, and loss as sources of stress. Finally, we will look more closely at the process of burnout and how to beat it. As you move through these studies, you will find help in managing the wear and tear of contemporary living.

LEADER: Be sure to read the "Questions and Answers" on pages 3–5. Take some time during this first session to have the group go over the ground rules on page 5. At the beginning of the Caring Time have your group look at pages M1–M3 in the center section of this book.

• Stress is known to be a major contributor, either directly or indirectly, of coronary heart disease, cancer, lung ailments, accidental injuries, cirrhosis of the liver and suicide—six of the leading causes of death in the U.S.

• It is estimated that two-thirds of office visits to family doctors are prompted by stress-related symptoms.

In this course, you will have a chance to look at six areas of your life and take an inventory in each area.

- Stress from worry
- Stress from work
- Stress from failure
- Stress from conflict
- Stress from loss
- Stress from overload

Every session has three parts: (1) **Ice-Breaker**—to break the ice and introduce the topic, (2) **Bible Study**—to share your life through a passage of Scripture, and (3) **Caring Time**—to share prayer concerns and pray for one another.

Ice-Breaker / 15 Minutes

TV Quiz Show. Like a TV quiz show, someone from the group picks a category and reads the four questions—pausing to let the others in the group guess before revealing the answer. When the first person is finished, everyone adds up the money they won by guessing right. Go around the group and have each person take a category. The person with the most money at the end wins.

CLOTHES

For $1: For clothes, I'm more likely to shop at:
❑ Sears
❑ Saks Fifth Avenue

For $2: I feel more comfortable wearing:
❑ formal clothes ❑ grubbies
❑ casual clothes ❑ sport clothes

For $3: In buying clothes, I look first for:
❑ fashion / style ❑ quality
❑ name brand ❑ price

For $4: In buying clothes, I usually:
❑ shop all day for a bargain
❑ choose one store, but try on everything
❑ buy the first thing I try on
❑ buy without trying on

FOOD

For $1: I prefer to eat at a:
❑ fast-food restaurant
❑ fancy restaurant

For $2: On the menu, I look for something:
❑ familiar ❑ way-out
❑ different

For $3: When eating chicken, my preference is a:
❑ drumstick ❑ wing
❑ breast ❑ gizzard

For $4: I draw the line when it comes to eating:
❑ frog legs
❑ snails
❑ raw oysters
❑ Rocky Mountain oysters

more on next page ⟶

TASTES

For $1: In music, I am closer to:
❒ Bach   ❒ Beatles

For $2: My choice of reading material is:
❒ science fiction   ❒ mystery
❒ sports   ❒ romance

For $3: In furniture, I prefer:
❒ Early American
❒ French Provincial
❒ Scandinavian—contemporary
❒ Hodgepodge—little of everything

For $4: If I had $1,000 to splurge, I would buy:
❒ one original painting
❒ two numbered prints
❒ three reproductions and an easy chair
❒ four cheap imitations and entertainment center

TRAVEL

For $1: When it comes to travel, I prefer:
❒ excitement   ❒ enrichment

For $2: On a vacation, my lifestyle is:
❒ go-go all the time ❒ slow and easy
❒ party every night and sleep in

For $3: In packing for a trip, I include:
❒ toothbrush and change of underwear
❒ light bag and good book
❒ small suitcase and nice outfit
❒ all but the kitchen sink

For $4: If I had money to blow, I would choose:
❒ one glorious night in a luxury hotel
❒ a weekend in a nice hotel
❒ a full week in a cheap hotel
❒ two weeks camping in boondocks

CARS

For $1: My car is likely to be:
❒ spotless   ❒ messy

For $2: The part of my car that I keep in the best condition is:
❒ interior   ❒ exterior
❒ engine

For $3: I am more likely to buy a:
❒ luxury car—10 mpg
❒ sports car—20 mpg
❒ economy car—30 mpg
❒ tiny car—40 mpg

For $4: If I had my choice of antique cars I would choose:
❒ 1937 silver Rolls Royce
❒ 1952 red MG convertible
❒ 1929 Model A Ford with rumble seat
❒ 1955 pink T-bird

HABITS

For $1: I am more likely to squeeze the toothpaste:
❒ in the middle   ❒ from the end

For $2: If I am lost, I will probably:
❒ stop and ask directions
❒ check the map
❒ find the way by driving around

For $3: I read the newspaper starting with the:
❒ front page
❒ entertainment section
❒ funnies
❒ sports

For $4: When I undress at night, I put my clothes:
❒ on a hanger in the closet
❒ folded neatly over a chair
❒ into a hamper or clothes basket
❒ on the floor

ENTERTAINMENT

For $1: I would likely:
☐ go out for a first-run movie
☐ stay home for a TV video

For $2: On TV, I would choose:
☐ soap opera   ☐ evening news
☐ Monday Night Football

For $3: If a movie gets scary, I usually:
☐ love it
☐ close my eyes
☐ go to the bathroom
☐ clutch a friend

For $4: Concerning movies, I prefer:
☐ romantic comedy   ☐ Walt Disney
☐ serious drama   ☐ action films
☐ science fiction

WORK

For $1: I prefer to work at a job that is:
☐ too big to handle
☐ too small to be challenging

For $2: The job I find most unpleasant:
☐ cleaning the house
☐ working in the yard
☐ balancing the checkbook

For $3: In choosing a job, I look for:
☐ salary
☐ working conditions
☐ security
☐ fulfillment

For $4: If I had to choose between these jobs, I would choose:
☐ pickle inspector at processing plant
☐ complaint officer at department store
☐ bedpan changer at hospital
☐ personnel manager in charge of fir-

Bible Study / 30 Minutes

Luke 10:38–42 / Too Busy

In this course, the Bible Study approach is a little unique with a different focus. Usually the focus of the Bible Study is the content of the passage. In this first session, the focus will be on telling your "story" using the passage as a springboard. In this passage, Jesus visits the home of his friends, Martha and Mary, and helps them establish healthy priorities. Read Luke 10:38–42 and discuss your responses to the following questions with your group. Be sure to save time at the close to discuss the issues in the CARING TIME.

> *38As Jesus and his disciples were on their way, he came to a village where a woman named Martha opened her home to him. 39She had a sister called Mary, who sat at the Lord's feet listening to what he said. 40But Martha was distracted by all the preparations that had to be made. She came to him and asked, "Lord, don't you care that my sister has left me to do the work by myself? Tell her to help me!"*

9

41 "Martha, Martha," the Lord answered, **"you are worried and upset about many things, 42but only one thing is needed. Mary has chosen what is better, and it will not be taken away from her."**

1. Growing up, who did you admire for the way they handled stress?
   - ❒ my mother
   - ❒ a grandparent
   - ❒ my pastor
   - ❒ another relative
   - ❒ a neighbor
   - ❒ my father
   - ❒ a brother/sister
   - ❒ a friend
   - ❒ a teacher
   - ❒ other:_____

2. Which of these situations quickly elevates your stress level?
   - ❒ a visit from a relative
   - ❒ seven straight days of rain
   - ❒ six hours in the car with my kids
   - ❒ my spouse asking me to help clean the house
   - ❒ my boss wanting to see me
   - ❒ sitting down to pay the monthly bills

3. Why do you think Martha drove herself like she did?
   - ❒ She had a desire to prove herself.
   - ❒ It was the only way she could feel good about herself.
   - ❒ She loved Jesus.
   - ❒ She wanted to make an impression on Jesus.
   - ❒ It was a way to make herself look better than her sister Mary.

4. What was Jesus saying to Martha?
   - ❒ She should chill out.
   - ❒ She should be more like Mary.
   - ❒ She could learn from Mary's different style.
   - ❒ She should be glad Mary had chosen to follow Christ.
   - ❒ "Sitting at Jesus' feet" is more important than anything else.
   - ❒ other:_____

5. How do you feel about Jesus' response to Martha?
   - ❒ irritated—It just shows that he was a man with male values.
   - ❒ disappointed—He should have sent Mary in to help, so both could return to listen later when the work was done.
   - ❒ ambivalent—I see his point, but I don't like it.
   - ❒ justified—He approved the course I would have taken.
   - ❒ enlightened—He affirmed her need to receive from God rather than to endlessly strive on her own.

6. How would you compare your work habits with Martha's habits?
- ❐ Our work habits are very similar.
- ❐ Martha is a lot more driven than I am.
- ❐ I'm a lot more driven than Martha.
- ❐ It all depends on what work I'm doing.

7. What "one thing is needed" for you to start taking the stress out of your life?
- ❐ I need to find a "Martha" to do all my work for me.
- ❐ I need to take on Mary's reflective, contemplative style.
- ❐ I need to learn more about Christ and what he thought was important in life.
- ❐ I need to be closer to Christ personally.
- ❐ other:_____

Caring Time / 15–45 Minutes

LEADER:
Ask the group, "Who are you going to invite next week?"

The most important time in every meeting is this—the CARING TIME—where you take time to share prayer requests and pray for one another. To make sure this time is not neglected, you need to set a minimum time that you will devote to prayer requests and prayer and count backwards from the closing time by this amount. For instance, if you are going to close at 9 p.m., and you are going to devote 30 minutes to prayer requests and prayer, you need to ask a timekeeper to call "time" at 8:30 and move to prayer requests. Start out by asking everyone to answer this question:

"How can we help you in prayer this week?"

Then, move into prayer. If you have not prayed out loud before, finish this sentence:

"Hello, God, this is ... (first name). I want to thank you for ..."

Be sure to pray for the empty chair. And as you do, think about who you could invite to join you as you begin this study.

GROUP
DIRECTORY

P.S.
At the close, pass around your books and have everyone sign the GROUP DIRECTORY inside the front cover.

SESSION
2

Stress From Worry

3-PART AGENDA

ICE-BREAKER
15 Minutes

BIBLE STUDY
30 Minutes

CARING TIME
15–45 Minutes

A few years ago, singer Bobby McFerrin sang a song called "Don't Worry, Be Happy." It was a simple little song, and its popularity was a testimony to the need of our modern world for its message. We live in a world that is filled with reasons to worry: escalating crime that is no longer just an inner city problem, guns in our schools, child abductions, glum predictions for the long-term health of our economy, ecological crises that threaten the planet, and more!

If we let ourselves become preoccupied with worry over all these things, we will drain ourselves of all our energy, with nothing left to enjoy the life that God has given us. But there is an alternative. In the midst of such complex problems, perhaps some Bible teachings might point the way to realizing the hope of McFerrin's simple song.

In this session, you will have a chance to deal with the problem of stress from worry in your life. There are two options for the Bible Study. Option 1—for beginner groups—starts with a familiar passage from the Sermon on the Mount about worry. Option 2—for deeper groups—starts with a passage from James that addresses believers who "face trials of many kinds."

> **LEADER:** *If there are new people in this session, review the ground rules for this group on page 5. Have the group look at page M4 in the center section and decide which Bible Study option to use— light or heavy. If you have more than seven people, see the box about the "Fearless Foursome" on page 4.*

James' focus is not on doctrine, but on how the Christian faith is to be lived on a day-to-day basis. Although Jesus is seldom referred to or quoted, his teaching on the Sermon on the Mount (Matthew 5–7) underlies much of his letter.

Be sure to save plenty of time in this session for the CARING TIME—to share your concerns and pray for one another. This is what this course is all about.

Ice-Breaker / 15 Minutes

My Worry History. Go around the group on the first question and share what caused your parents a lot of worry. If you have time left over, go around again on as much of question 2 as you have time for.

1. During your childhood, what do you remember your parents worrying about? (Check those that apply.)

___ money   ___ job / busines
___ health   ___ taxes
___ house payment   ___ problem children
___ war / peace   ___ politics
___ family conflict   ___ weather
___ crime   ___ the Depression / economy

2. Which two areas of your life were of most concern to you five years ago? Which two were most worrisome 12 months ago? Which two did you find yourself worrying about only last week? Do you find any continuity of concern from year to year, week to week? What does that tell you?

___ job / business   ___ sex   ___ money
___ marriage   ___ parents   ___ politics
___ health   ___ relationships   ___ fulfillment
___ children   ___ spiritual life   ___ retirement

Bible Study / 30 Minutes

Option 1 / Gospel Study

Matthew 6:25–34 / Worry Warts

Read Matthew 6:25–34 and discuss your responses to the following questions with your group. This Bible passage is taken from the Sermon on the Mount, which Jesus shared with his followers.

25 "Therefore I tell you, do not worry about your life, what you will eat or drink; or about your body, what you will wear. Is not life more important than food, and the body more important than clothes? 26 Look at the birds of the air; they do not sow or reap or store away in barns, and yet your heavenly Father feeds them. Are you not much more valuable than they? 27 Who of you by worrying can add a single hour to his life?

28 "And why do you worry about clothes? See how the lilies of the field grow. They do not labor or spin. [29] Yet I tell you that not even Solomon in all his splendor was dressed like one of these. [30] If that is how God clothes the grass of the field, which is here today and tomorrow is thrown into the fire, will he not much more clothe you, O you of little faith? [31] So do not worry, saying, 'What shall we eat?' or 'What shall we drink?' or 'What shall we wear?' [32] For the pagans run after all these things, and your heavenly Father knows that you need them. [33] But seek first his kingdom and his righteousness, and all these things will be given to you as well. [34] Therefore do not worry about tomorrow, for tomorrow will worry about itself. Each day has enough trouble of its own."

"Worry does not empty tomorrow of its sorrow; it empties today of its strength."
—Corrie ten Boom

1. If you had heard this passage for the first time (and did not know that Jesus said it), what would have been your first reaction?
❒ Sounds like a hippy from the '60s.
❒ This person is out of touch with the modern world.
❒ This guy doesn't have to support a family.
❒ This is the kind of message our world needs.
❒ I wish it were that easy.

2. When Jesus said, "Do not worry about your life," he meant:
❒ Live one day at a time.
❒ Don't plan for tomorrow.
❒ Trusting God is an important part of planning for tomorrow.
❒ God will take care of us, no matter what we do.
❒ Worry is a waste of time and energy.

3. What issues cause you the most concern?
❒ bills and having enough money to pay them
❒ my job and how secure it is
❒ whether I'll ever marry
❒ whether we can stay married
❒ my children's safety, or whether they will ever "amount to much of anything"
❒ the economy, or whether the stock market will crash
❒ the lack of world peace
❒ other:_____

4. How do you usually handle worry?
❒ What, me worry?
❒ I talk about it so much that others worry.
❒ I get busy so I don't think about it.
❒ I let go and let God take care of it.
❒ I worry so much it worries me.
❒ I give in to one of my vices to relieve the pressure.
❒ I get professional help.
❒ other:_____

14

5. If you could choose to live a simple life (like the Waltons) with few amenities and fewer debts, would you do it?

6. If you could change one thing that causes you to worry, what would it be?
- ❐ my need to impress others
- ❐ overspending
- ❐ my priorities in life
- ❐ other: _____
- ❐ expectations that I put on myself and others

7. If Jesus could have five minutes with you today, what would he say?
- ❐ Learn to laugh more at your troubles.
- ❐ Learn to live one day at a time.
- ❐ Get out of the situation you're in.
- ❐ Take time to smell the flowers.
- ❐ Lower the expectations you've placed on yourself and others.
- ❐ Simplify your lifestyle.
- ❐ Focus more on God's kingdom and less on this one.
- ❐ other:_____

Option 2 / Epistle Study

James 1:2–11 / Winning Over Worry

Have someone in your group read James 1:2–11 and then discuss the questions that follow. If you do not understand a word or phrase, check the reference notes after the questions.

²Consider it pure joy, my brothers, whenever you face trials of many kinds, ³because you know that the testing of your faith develops perseverance. ⁴Perseverance must finish its work so that you may be mature and complete, not lacking anything. ⁵If any of you lacks wisdom, he should ask God, who gives generously to all without finding fault, and it will be given to him. ⁶But when he asks, he must believe and not doubt, because he who doubts is like a wave of the sea, blown and tossed by the wind. ⁷That man should not think he will receive anything from the Lord; ⁸he is a double-minded man, unstable in all he does.

⁹The brother in humble circumstances ought to take pride in his high position. ¹⁰But the one who is rich should take pride in his low position, because he will pass away like a wild flower. ¹¹For the sun rises with scorching heat and withers the plant; its blossom falls and its beauty is destroyed. In the same way, the rich man will fade away even while he goes about his business.

1. Who is the "tower of strength" in your family during hard times?

2. According to James, what should our attitude be when facing trials? How often is this *your* attitude in stressful times?

3. Why should anyone feel joyful about trials and hard times? What are the potential benefits of such times?

4. How is true wisdom obtained (v. 5)?

5. When asking God for guidance, what must we guard against?

6. What do you do when you are going through something terribly stressful and you want to trust God's wisdom, but you have doubts?

7. According to verses 9–11, why do the humble occupy a high position and the rich a low position?

8. According to this passage, how can you win over the worries that come with hard times, the lack of wisdom, and the lack of money?

Caring Time / 15–45 Minutes

Take time at the close to share any personal prayer requests. Answer the question:

"How can we help you in prayer this week?"

LEADER:
Ask the group, "Who are you going to invite next week?"

Then go around and let each person pray for the person on their right. Finish this sentence:

"Our Father, I want to speak to you about my friend _____."

During your prayer time, remember to pray for the empty chair and for the growth of your group.

Reference Notes

Summary. James begins by laying out in their basic form the three themes he will discuss: testing, wisdom and riches. These themes are, in fact, connected. In order to survive the test, wisdom from God is needed. The nature of this test involves how riches are used. James uses verbal echoes to link together this section—verses 2 and 4 are connected by the repeated word *perseverance*. Verses 2–4 are linked to verses 5–8 by the word *lack*. The word *ask* is repeated in verses 5 and 6. The word *pride* links verses 9 and 10.

1:2–8 In this first paragraph, it is clear that James is discussing themes that parallel those in the Sermon on the Mount. Here he discusses joy in the midst of trial (Matt. 5:10–12); the exhortation to perfection (Matt. 5:48); and the request for good gifts (Matt. 7:7–11).

1:2–4 Here is the first theme James will treat in his epistle: the nature and value of trials and testing. This is a common theme in Christian ethical instruction (see Rom. 5:3–4 and 1 Peter 1:6–7). This theme is also found occasionally in the Old Testament (e.g., Gen. 22, Ps. 119:71, and the book of Job), though as Bacon remarked somewhat facetiously, "Prosperity is the blessing of the Old Testament, adversity the blessing of the New!"

1:2 *Consider it pure joy.* James says that Christians ought to view the difficulties of life with enthusiasm, because the outcome of trials will be beneficial. Such joy is not just a feeling, however. It is a form of activity. It is an active acceptance of adversity.

my brothers. James is addressing his letter to those who are members of the church. This is not a letter for the world at large. The phrase "my brothers" carries with a sense of warmth. Even though in the course of his letter James will say very harsh things to these brothers and sisters, it is never with the sense that they are despised or even different from him (see 3:1–2). This is family! "My brothers" is a recurrent phrase in James, often used when a new subject is introduced (e.g., 1:2,19; 2:14; 3:1; 5:7).

trials of many kinds. The word *trials* has the dual sense of "adversity" on the one hand (e.g., disease, persecution, tragedy) and "temptations" on the other hand (e.g., lust, greed, trust in wealth)—i.e., "pleasant allurements of Satan or painful afflictions of the body (that) are apt to lead men to sin" (Adamson). James is not urging Christians to seek trials. Trials will come on their own. This is simply the way life is, especially it seems for a first-century Christian whose church is being persecuted.

1:3 One reason that the Christian can rejoice in suffering is because immediate good does come out of the pain. In this verse, James assumes that there will be good results.

perseverance. Or *endurance* (sticking it out). The word is used in the sense of active overcoming, rather than passive acceptance. This is a virtue vital to the Christian life and comes mainly out of the trials, it seems.

1:4 *finish its work.* Perfection is not automatic; it takes time and effort.

mature and complete. What James has in mind here is wholeness of character. He is not calling for some sort of esoteric perfection or sinlessness. Instead, the emphasis is on moral blamelessness. He is thinking of the integrated life, in contrast to the divided person of verses 6–8. To be mature is to have reached a certain stage or to have fulfilled a given purpose. An animal had to be fully developed to be fit for sacrifice to God. To be complete is to have no flaws or blemishes. Trials produce this sort of maturity by blowing away "the chaff of error, hypocrisy, and doubt, leaving that which survives the test, viz. *the genuine element of true character*" (Adamson).

lacking. The opposite of mature and complete. This is a word used of an army that has been defeated or a person who has failed to reach a certain standard.

1:5–8 Wisdom is needed in order to deal with trials so that they produce wholeness of character. Wisdom is needed to understand how to consider such adversity pure joy. Wisdom is the second theme that James will treat in his book.

1:5 *wisdom.* This is not just abstract knowledge, but rather God-given insight which leads to right living. It is the ability to make right decisions, especially about moral issues (as one is called upon to do during trials).

generously. A reference both to the abundance of the gift and the spirit with which it is given. God gives fully, without hesitation and without grudging (see 2 Cor. 8:1–2).

ask God. See Matthew 7:7.

1:6 James now contrasts the lack of hesitation on God's part to give (v. 5) with the hesitation on people's part to ask (v. 6). Both here and in James 4:3, unanswered prayer is connected to the quality of the asking, not to the unwillingness of God to give.

believe. To be in *one mind* about God's ability to answer prayer, to be sure that God will hear and will act in accord with his superior wisdom. The ability to pray this sort of trusting prayer is an example of the character that is produced by trials.

1:8 *double-minded.* To doubt is to be in *two minds*—to believe and to disbelieve simultaneously; to be torn between two impulses—one positive, one negative (see James 4:8). This is epitomized perhaps by Augustine's prayer: "O Lord, grant me purity, but not yet."

unstable. "The man who is divided in himself, then, will show himself as such in his doubtful prayer, and also in his inability to act firmly or reliably" (Laws).

1:9–11 Poverty is an example of a trial to be endured—but so too are riches, though in quite a different way. The question of riches and poverty is the third major theme in the book of James.

1:9 *humble circumstances.* Those who are poor in a material and social sense, and who are looked down on by others because they are poor.

take pride. Such boasting is equivalent to the rejoicing that is encouraged in verse 2 in the face of adversity. Such an uncharacteristic attitude can only occur when the poor see beyond immediate circumstances to the fact of their new position as children of God. While they may be poor in worldly goods, they are rich beyond imagining since they are children of God and thus heirs of the whole world. Therefore, they do in fact have a superior position in life and ought to rejoice in it.

high position. In the early church, the poor gained a new, quite remarkable sense of self-respect. The slave found that traditional social distinctions had been obliterated (Gal. 3:28). A slave might minister to a congregation in which his or her master sat. In Christ, slaves found a God-given purpose. They were not useless. The judgment of society on them was not accurate.

1:10 *rich.* The peril of riches is that people come to trust in wealth as a source of security. It is a mark of double-mindedness to attempt to serve both God and money. In James, the word rich "always indicates one outside the community, a nonbelieving person. The rich, in fact, are the oppressors of the community (2:6; 5:1–6)" (Davids, GNC).

low position. Jewish culture understood wealth to be a sure sign of God's favor. Here, as elsewhere (vv. 2,9) James reverses conventional expectations.

wild flower. In February, spring comes to Palestine with a blaze of color, as flowers like the lily, the poppy and the lupine blossom appear along with a carpet of grass. By May, however, all the flowers and grass are brown.

1:11 *scorching heat.* The hot, southeast desert wind (the sirocco) sweeps into Palestine in the spring "like a blast of hot air when an oven door is opened" (Barclay). It blows day and night until the verdant cover is withered and brown.

fade away. Wealth gives an uncertain security, since it is apt to be swept away as abruptly as desert flowers (see Isa. 40:6–8).

GROUP DIRECTORY

P.S.
If you have a new person in your group, be sure to add their name to the group directory inside the front cover.

SESSION

3

Stress From Work

3-PART AGENDA

ICE-BREAKER
15 Minutes

BIBLE STUDY
30 Minutes

CARING TIME
15–45 Minutes

Work holds a central place in the lives of many of us. And we work for many different reasons. Most basically, we work to survive. We may also work to give our children and grandchildren a better life. Others of us work primarily to obtain material goods. And ideally, all of us would like to be involved in work that is "meaningful."

While work can certainly be satisfying, it can also be stressful. An excessive workload, an unreasonable boss, monotonous work, and job insecurity are just a few of the stresses faced in the workplace. How you handle the stresses from your work can directly affect other areas of your life.

The "flipside" of work stress is experienced by the workaholic. The workaholic thrives on work and often experiences stress when she/he is away from work. Workaholism also directly affects other areas of a person's life.

LEADER: If there are more than seven people at this meeting, divide into groups of 4 for Bible Study. Count off around the group: "one, two, one, two, etc."—and have the "ones" quickly move to another room. When you come back together for the Caring Time, have the group read about your Mission on page M5 of the center section.

The issue is one of balance. Too little work or meaningless work destroys our sense of worth; too much work or overly demanding work destroys our bodies and psyches. Both extremes cause stress.

The following Bible studies will look at the relationship between work and stress. In Option 1, we will look at a parable Jesus told about an employer, and we will have a chance to consider issues like fair pay. In Option 2, we will look at stress from overwork, and the issue of the meaning of work. We will do so by considering an apparent workaholic named Paul.

Remember, the purpose of the Bible Study is to share your own story. Use this opportunity to deal with some issues in your life. The ice-breaker is just for fun and should not last more than 15 minutes. Be sure to save time at the close for prayer requests and prayer.

Ice-Breaker / 15 Minutes

Employment Office. Read the list of job openings aloud and quickly choose someone in your group for each job—based upon their unique gifts and talents. Have fun!

SPACE ENVIRONMENTAL ENGINEER—in charge of designing the bathrooms on space shuttles

SCHOOL BUS DRIVER—for junior high kids in New York City (earplugs supplied)

CHARM SCHOOL OPERATOR—for Harley-Davidson bikers

NEWSPAPER COLUMN WRITER—of "advice to the lovelorn"

COMPLAINT DEPARTMENT SUPERVISOR—for a large automobile dealership and service department

PET PSYCHIATRIST—for French poodles in Beverly Hills

SAFARI GUIDE—in the heart of Africa, for wealthy widows and eccentric bachelors

LITTLE LEAGUE BASEBALL COACH—in Mudville, Illinois; last year's record was 0 and 12

FAST-FOOD MANAGER—of your local McDonald's, during the summer with 210 teenage employees

OFFICIAL PHYSICIAN—for the National Association of Hypochondriacs

TOY ASSEMBLY PERSON—for a toy store over the holidays

CHOREOGRAPHER—for the Dallas Cowboys cheerleaders

NURSE'S AIDE—at a home for retired Sumo wrestlers

Bible Study / 30 Minutes

Option 1 / Gospel Study

Matthew 20:1–16 / Stress in the Workplace

Read Matthew 20:1–16 and discuss your responses to the following questions with your group. This is one of many parables that Jesus told about the spiritual kingdom which God was setting up.

20 *"For the kingdom of heaven is like a landowner who went out early in the morning to hire men to work in his vineyard. ²He agreed to pay them a denarius for the day and sent them into his vineyard.*

³"About the third hour he went out and saw others standing in the marketplace doing nothing. ⁴He told them, 'You also go and work in my vineyard, and I will pay you whatever is right.' ⁵So they went.

"He went out again about the sixth hour and the ninth hour and did the same thing. ⁶About the eleventh hour he went out and found still others standing around. He asked them, 'Why have you been standing here all day long doing nothing?'

⁷" 'Because no one has hired us,' they answered.

"He said to them, 'You also go and work in my vineyard.'

⁸"When evening came, the owner of the vineyard said to his foreman, 'Call the workers and pay them their wages, beginning with the last ones hired and going on to the first.'

⁹"The workers who were hired about the eleventh hour came and each received a denarius. ¹⁰So when those came who were hired first, they expected to receive more. But each one of them also received a denarius. ¹¹When they received it, they began to grumble against the landowner. ¹²'These men who were hired last worked only one hour,' they said, 'and you have made them equal to us who have borne the burden of the work and the heat of the day.'

¹³"But he answered one of them, 'Friend, I am not being unfair to you. Didn't you agree to work for a denarius? ¹⁴Take your pay and go. I want to give the man who was hired last the same as I gave you. ¹⁵Don't I have the right to do what I want with my own money? Or are you envious because I am generous?'

¹⁶"So the last will be first, and the first will be last."

1. If someone had told you this story during coffee break at work, what would have been your first reaction?

❐ This is a fantasy world.

❐ Those last guys must have had a good union.

❐ Where do I sign up to work for that guy?

❐ Typical boss—seniority means nothing.

❐ He's the boss—he can do whatever he wants.

2. If you were one of the first workers hired, how would you have reacted to the landowner?

❐ I would have complained about him behind his back.

❐ I wouldn't have complained, because I got the pay I agreed to.

❐ I would have reported him to the Jerusalem Better Business Bureau.

❐ I would never work for him again.

❐ I would have been happy for the workers hired after I was.

3. What were the unmet expectations of the first workers, which created a conflict with the landowner?
   ❐ They expected more money for more work.
   ❐ They expected to get paid for doing little work.
   ❐ They expected the landowner to be fair.
   ❐ They expected the landowner to do whatever he wanted.

4. What was your very first job? How much money did you make?

5. Which employer has been the most generous in their compensation to you? The most stingy?

6. What expectations regarding compensation do you have of your employer?
   ❐ If I go the "extra mile," I expect to be rewarded.
   ❐ No matter what I do, I will get paid the same.
   ❐ I work for rewards other than money.
   ❐ Employers are never fair and never will be.
   ❐ I expect equal pay for equal work.

7. What is the main reason you work?
   ❐ to survive
   ❐ to give our children and grandchildren a better life
   ❐ to obtain material goods
   ❐ because I'd be bored otherwise
   ❐ because work is fulfilling

8. While work can certainly be satisfying, it can also be stressful. Which of the following do you consider to be the most stressful in the workplace?
   ❐ an excessive workload   ❐ job insecurity
   ❐ an unreasonable boss   ❐ irritating coworkers
   ❐ monotonous work   ❐ poor pay / benefits
   ❐ balancing work with the rest of life   ❐ other:_____

COMMENT

This is a parable about a "large-hearted man who is compassionate and full of sympathy for the poor" (Jeremias). "The essential point of the parable is that God is like that; his generosity transcends human ideas of fairness. No one receives less than they deserve, but some receive far more" (R.T. France).

We learn from this parable that God's standards are not our standards. Hard work and high reward are not equal in his kingdom. After all, it is all grace. We also note that the work-related stress in this passage is a matter of an understandable (but harmful) *attitude*. The stress does not come

23

because the workers are cheated by the boss; everyone gets a fair wage. The stress comes from jealousy—some get the same wage for less work than others. Sometimes it is our attitude that needs changing in order to relieve stress. Even in an exploitative situation, the answer may be to change our attitude in various ways: to confront the problem regardless of cost, to deal directly and openly instead of backbiting, and to find our own satisfaction in the job.

Option 2 / Epistle Study

2 Corinthians 11:16–33 / The Workaholic

Read 2 Corinthians 11:16–33 and share your responses to the following questions with your group. This is taken from the writings of the apostle Paul, who is defending his life and work.

[16]*I repeat: Let no one take me for a fool. But if you do, then receive me just as you would a fool, so that I may do a little boasting.* [17]*In this self-confident boasting I am not talking as the Lord would, but as a fool.* [18]*Since many are boasting in the way the world does, I too will boast.* [19]*You gladly put up with fools since you are so wise!* [20]*In fact, you even put up with anyone who enslaves you or exploits you or takes advantage of you or pushes himself forward or slaps you in the face.* [21]*To my shame I admit that we were too weak for that!*

What anyone else dares to boast about—I am speaking as a fool—I also dare to boast about. [22]*Are they Hebrews? So am I. Are they Israelites? So am I. Are they Abraham's descendants? So am I.* [23]*Are they servants of Christ? (I am out of my mind to talk like this.) I am more. I have worked much harder, been in prison more frequently, been flogged more severely, and been exposed to death again and again.* [24]*Five times I received from the Jews the forty lashes minus one.* [25]*Three times I was beaten with rods, once I was stoned, three times I was shipwrecked, I spent a night and a day in the open sea,* [26]*I have been constantly on the move. I have been in danger from rivers, in danger from bandits, in danger from my own countrymen, in danger from Gentiles; in danger in the city, in danger in the country, in danger at sea; and in danger from false brothers.* [27]*I have labored and toiled and have often gone without sleep; I have known hunger and thirst and have often gone without food; I have been cold and naked.* [28]*Besides everything else, I face daily the pressure of my concern for all the churches.* [29]*Who is weak, and I do not feel weak? Who is led into sin, and I do not inwardly burn?*

[30]*If I must boast, I will boast of the things that show my weakness.* [31]*The God and Father of the Lord Jesus, who is to be praised forever, knows*

that I am not lying. [32]In Damascus the governor under King Aretas had the city of the Damascenes guarded in order to arrest me. [33]But I was lowered in a basket from a window in the wall and slipped through his hands.

1. Why would the apostle Paul resort to boasting (see Summary in the notes)?

2. Of the four temperaments, which temperament describes Paul best?

   SANGUINE: Super salesperson. Warm. Outgoing. Happy-go-lucky on the surface. Charmer.

   CHOLERIC: Super leader. Assertive. Self-willed driver. Crusader. Task-oriented. Entrepreneur.

   MELANCHOLIC: Super sensitive. Creative. Imaginative. Lover of peace and quiet. Artistic.

   PHLEGMATIC: Super laid-back. Likable. Dependable. Practical. Conservative. Easygoing.

3. Why do you think Paul drove himself like he did?

4. How would you like to have Paul as your boss? As your employee?

5. How would you compare your work habits with Paul's?

6. At work, which temperament described in question #2 sounds most like you?

7. What advice do you think Paul would give you about dealing with the stress you face in your work?

8. On the following scale, how would you evaluate the amount of time and emotional energy you give to work?

1	2	3	4	5	6	7	8	9	10
far too little				just right					far too much

9. On the following scale, how would you evaluate the amount of meaning you get out of work?

1	2	3	4	5	6	7	8	9	10
far too little				just right					far too much

Caring Time / 15–45 Minutes

LEADER:
Ask the group, "Who are you going to invite next week?"

Take some time to share any personal prayer requests and answer the question:

"If you knew you could not fail, what would you like to change about your work or career?"

Close with a short time of prayer, remembering the dreams that have been shared. If you would like to pray in silence, say the word "Amen" when you have finished your prayer, so that the next person will know when to start.

Reference Notes

Summary. In 2 Corinthians 11:1–15, Paul pinpointed the danger that certain false apostles pose to the Corinthian church. They are, in fact, preaching a different Jesus, a different spirit, and a different gospel (11:4). They are getting away with this because of their supposed qualifications "which, we may deduce from the letter as a whole, consisted of commendation from high authority, impressive speech and behaviour, and manifestations of the Spirit, and Paul, seeing the peril of the Corinthian church, decides, against his will, to beat them at their own game" (Barrett). Thus, Paul boasts of his own credentials! Interestingly, because he does so, we catch a glimpse of the life he lived as an apostle. Paul began to speak about boasting in verse 1 but got sidetracked. Now he picks up this theme again. Although such boasting is distasteful to him, he is forced to demonstrate that in no way (heritage, calling, sacrifice for the Gospel) are the false apostles superior to him.

11:16 *take me for a fool.* Although Paul is forced to boast, he is not so deceived as to think that in this way he can really demonstrate superiority. Boasting is not the path to true wisdom. It is a temporary expedient forced on him, and he knows it.

11:18 Such boasting is more characteristic of the world (which leaves God out of the picture) than it is of God's servants.

11:19 The Corinthians tolerate fools out of an attitude of superiority.

11:20 Despite thinking themselves to be wise, they, in fact, allow themselves to be grossly misused by pompous teachers. In fact, in a curious way it was because of the very arrogant, demanding manner of these teachers that they accepted them as true apostles.

put up with. The Corinthians seem quite willing to submit to all manner of arrogant manipulation by these false teachers.

enslaves. The Judaizers led people into a severe bondage to the Law, requiring not only circumcision but the observance of countless petty regulations.

exploits. Jewish rabbis were not allowed to accept pay for their teaching and, theoretically, were supposed to work. But, in fact, it was also taught that "it was work of exceptional merit to support a rabbi and that he who did so made sure of a place in the heavenly academy" (Barclay). Thus some teachers became quite greedy and exploitive.

pushes himself forward. In fact some rabbis became quite arrogant, demanding more respect than that given even to one's parents.

slaps you in the face. This may be meant literally (see Acts 23:2) or may be a metaphor for the insulting behavior of the teachers.

11:21 weak. In contrast to the assertive confidence of the false apostles stands Paul's own weakness: "weakness" that refuses to exploit others because that is not the Gospel way.

11:22 Paul begins his boasting by pointing out that by any manner of reckoning he is as Jewish as it is possible to be; i.e., the false apostles from Jerusalem cannot claim to be better Jews than he—which would undercut their claim to be preaching a "purer" gospel.

Hebrews. Paul is a pure-blooded Jew. He is not a convert or a half-Jew (with only one Jewish parent). He may also be using this term (rather than simply calling himself a "Jew") to indicate that he speaks Hebrew over against the Hellenized Jews who adopted the Greek culture and language.

Israelites. Furthermore, he was brought up in the Jewish religion and culture.

Abraham's descendants. Here the emphasis is on the fact that such folk are part of God's chosen people. They are what they are because of God's special call to them.

11:23–28 Having listed his Jewish credentials, Paul next turns to his qualifications as a Christian: he has suffered greatly as the servant of Christ. As a pioneer missionary his life has been fraught with danger and toil. The accounts in Acts give sketchy information about Paul, so it is not always possible to know specifically to what Paul refers in each incident.

11:25 beaten with rods. This is how the Romans administered punishment (e.g., Acts 16:22–23).

stoned. See, for example, Acts 14:19.

shipwrecked. See Acts 27:14–44 for the story of a shipwreck—though that particular incident had not yet occurred at the time Paul wrote 2 Corinthians. Since Paul traveled frequently by ship, and since shipwrecks were by no means uncommon in those days, it seems that Paul endured at least two shipwrecks.

11:26 Having recalled the shipwreck, Paul now goes on to describe other dangers that lay in wait of travelers.

rivers. Not all rivers had bridges or safe ferries.

bandits. This would have been a special problem when Paul was transporting collections taken in aid of poorer churches.

in danger from my own countrymen. Such danger came from mobs, from the courts, and from personal attack (see Acts 9:23,29; 13:8,45; 14:2,19; 17:5; 18:6,12; 20:3,19; 21:11,27).

in danger from Gentiles. See Acts 16:20; 19:23–31.

in danger from false brothers. Not only did he face the possibility of harm (bodily and otherwise) from Jews and Gentiles, but also from so-called Christians!

11:29 weak. Paul's emphasis throughout this section has been on his weakness—his unimpressive speech, his poor appearance, his poverty—in which he glories because thus is Christ's power revealed. In his "boasting" he now boasts of being weakest of all!

inwardly burn. In his concern for the churches, a constant source of anguish is over those who have been led astray from the faith.

11:31 It might seem so incongruous that one could be both an apostle and a suffering servant that Paul asserts he has indeed been telling the truth in the preceding descriptions.

11:32 Almost as if to illustrate once more that trial and humiliation make up the life of an apostle, Paul recounts one last story.

King Aretas. An Arab king who ruled from 9 B.C. to A.D. 39.

SESSION

4

Stress From Failure

3-PART AGENDA

ICE-BREAKER
15 Minutes

BIBLE STUDY
30 Minutes

CARING TIME
15–45 Minutes

Our society rewards success and punishes failure. There is great pressure to make it, to do it right, to be together. We love winners; we shun losers. As a result, we grow up with a deep need to succeed. From Little League baseball to grades in school to competition in the fine arts to acceptance in the best colleges the message is the same: making it is what life is all about. Not surprisingly, stress is connected with avoiding failure.

All of us have failed at some time or another. Failure really isn't much fun. But if we fear failure, we can be immobilized and will avoid anything that involves a degree of risk. We can learn much through failure. Often failure is a prerequisite to success.

The stories of successful people invariably tell us that they have failed one or more times before they became successful. Abraham Lincoln considered himself to be a failure in the eyes of his contemporaries. Thomas Edison failed repeatedly before he lit his first incandescent bulb. Marie Curie (inventor of the X-ray) persevered despite financial, scientific and health setbacks. Winston Churchill helps to give us a perspective on failure when he said, "Success is going from failure to failure without loss of enthusiasm."

LEADER: If you have a new person at this session, remember to use Option 1 rather than Option 2 for the Bible Study. During the Caring Time, don't forget to keep praying for the empty chair.

In the Option 1 Bible Study (from Luke's Gospel), Peter painfully learns some deeper truths through failure. In the Option 2 Bible Study (from Romans), the apostle Paul experiences some failure in his inward battle between good and evil. Both studies will help us rise above failure.

Ice-Breaker / 15 Minutes

How Is It With Your Soul? John Wesley, the founder of the Methodist Church, asked his "class meetings" to check in each week at their small group meeting with this question: "How is it with your soul?" To answer this question, choose one of these four allegories to explain the past week in your life:

WEATHER: For example: "This week has been mostly cloudy, with some thunderstorms at midweek. Right now, the weather is a little brighter ..."

MUSIC: For example: "This past week has been like heavy rock music—almost too loud. The sound seems to reverberate off the walls."

COLOR: For example: "This past week has been mostly fall colors— deep orange, flaming red and pumpkin."

SEASON OF THE YEAR: For example: "The season this past week has been like springtime. New signs of life are beginning to appear on the barren trees, and a few shoots of winter wheat are breaking through the frozen ground."

Bible Study / 30 Minutes

Option 1 / Gospel Study

Luke 22:54–62 / Career Crisis

Read Luke 22:54–62 and discuss your responses to the following questions with your group. This story describes the experience of one of Jesus' disciples on the night that Jesus was arrested and taken away to be tried and then crucified.

⁵⁴Then seizing him [Jesus], they [the temple police] led him away and took him into the house of the high priest. Peter followed at a distance. ⁵⁵But when they had kindled a fire in the middle of the courtyard and had sat down together, Peter sat down with them. ⁵⁶A servant girl saw him seated there in the firelight. She looked closely at him and said, "This man was with him."

⁵⁷But he denied it. "Woman, I don't know him," he said.

⁵⁸A little later someone else saw him and said, "You also are one of them."
"Man, I am not!" Peter replied.

⁵⁹About an hour later another asserted, "Certainly this fellow was with him, for he is a Galilean."

⁶⁰Peter replied, "Man, I don't know what you're talking about!" Just as he was speaking, the rooster crowed. ⁶¹The Lord turned and looked straight at Peter. Then Peter remembered the word the Lord had spoken to him: "Before the rooster crows today, you will disown me three times." ⁶²And he went outside and wept bitterly.

1. If you could put in a good word for Peter from this event, what would it be?
   ❏ He meant well.
   ❏ He was only human.
   ❏ At least he followed Jesus to his trial.
   ❏ He was confused.
   ❏ He came back to Christ in the end.
   ❏ other: _____

2. If you were in Peter's shoes, how would you have reacted?
   ❏ I would have kept my mouth shut.
   ❏ I would have gone home.
   ❏ I would have done the same as Peter.
   ❏ I would have argued Jesus' case.
   ❏ other: _____

3. How do you think Peter felt when Jesus looked at him?
   ❏ He realized how stupid he had been.
   ❏ He felt ashamed of his behavior.
   ❏ He was unaffected by the whole matter.
   ❏ He was humiliated by his failure.
   ❏ He was afraid Jesus would never forgive him.

4. What chance would you have given Peter after this event to make a comeback and go on to become a great leader?
   ❏ absolutely none
   ❏ not much
   ❏ maybe a little

"Often we assume that God is unable to work in spite of our weaknesses, mistakes, and sins. We forget that God is a specialist; he is able to work our failures into his plans."
—Erwin W. Lutzer

5. How do you generally react when you experience failure?
- ❏ I kick myself for days.
- ❏ I try to make up for it.
- ❏ I try to learn from my failures.
- ❏ I try to ignore and forget my failures.
- ❏ I accept failure as a reality of life and move on.
- ❏ I don't want to try again when I fail.
- ❏ I refuse to accept failure in anything I do.
- ❏ other:_____

6. How has failure in your life changed you?
- ❏ I'm emotionally fragile.
- ❏ I'm more determined.
- ❏ I'm more humble.
- ❏ I'm more realistic.
- ❏ I look out for myself more.
- ❏ I'm more sensitive to other people's pain.
- ❏ other: _____

7. What lesson or principle would you like to pass on to your kids (or to other people) in dealing with failure?

Option 2 / Epistle Study

Romans 7:7–25 / Fail-Safe

Read Romans 7:7–25 and discuss your responses to the following questions with your group. This in-depth passage talks about the relative roles of the Jewish Law. It also highlights God's forgiveness and grace in bringing people into a healing relationship with himself.

⁷What shall we say, then? Is the law sin? Certainly not! Indeed I would not have known what sin was except through the law. For I would not have known what coveting really was if the law had not said, "Do not covet." ⁸But sin, seizing the opportunity afforded by the commandment, produced in me every kind of covetous desire. For apart from law, sin is dead. ⁹Once I was alive apart from law; but when the commandment came, sin sprang to life and I died. ¹⁰I found that the very commandment that was intended to bring life actually brought death. ¹¹For sin, seizing the opportunity afforded by the commandment, deceived me, and through the commandment put me to death. ¹²So then, the law is holy, and the commandment is holy, righteous and good.

¹³Did that which is good, then, become death to me? By no means! But in order that sin might be recognized as sin, it produced death in me through

Leadership Training Supplement

YOU ARE
HERE

BIRTH	GROWTH	RELEASE
101	201	301

What is the game plan for your group in the 101 stage?

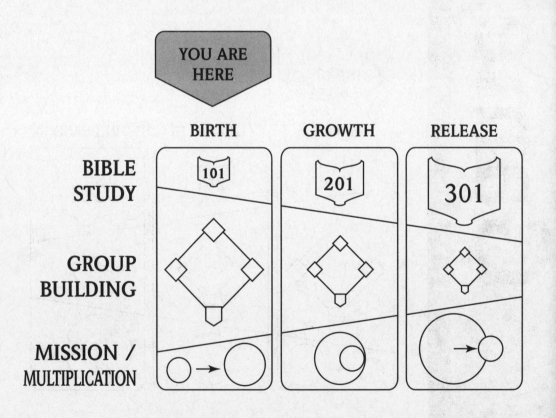

YOU ARE HERE

	BIRTH	GROWTH	RELEASE
BIBLE STUDY	101	201	301
GROUP BUILDING			
MISSION / MULTIPLICATION			

The 3-Legged Stool

The three essentials in a healthy small group are Bible Study, Group Building and Mission / Multiplication. You need all three to stay balanced—like a 3-legged stool.

- To focus only on Bible Study will lead to scholasticism.
- To focus only on Group Building will lead to narcissism.
- To focus only on Mission will lead to burnout.

You need a game plan for the life cycle of the group where all three of these elements are present in a mission-driven strategy. In the first stage of the group, here is the game plan.

Bible Study

To share your spiritual story through Scripture.

The greatest gift you can give a group is the gift of your spiritual story—the story of your spiritual beginnings, your spiritual growing pains, struggles, hopes and fears. The Bible Study is designed to help you tell your spiritual story to the group.

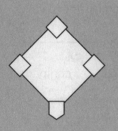

Group Building

To become a caring community.

In the first stage of a group, note how the baseball diamond is larger than the book and the circles. This is because Group Building is the priority in the first stage. Group Building is a four-step process to become a close-knit group. Using the baseball diamond illustration, the goal of Group Building—bonding—is home plate. But to get there you have to go around the bases.

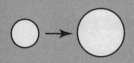

Mission / Multiplication

To grow your group numerically and spiritually.

The mission of your group is the greatest mission anyone can give their life to—to bring new people into a personal relationship with Christ and the fellowship of a Christian community. This purpose will become more prominent in the second and third stages of your group. In this stage, the goal is to invite new people into your group and try to double.

M3

Bible Study

In the first stage of a group, the Bible Study is where you get to know each other and share your spiritual stories. The Bible Study is designed to give the leader the option of going LIGHT or HEAVY, depending on the background of the people in the group. TRACK 1 is especially designed for beginner groups who do not know a lot about the Bible or each other. TRACK 2 is for groups who are familiar with the Bible and with one another.

Track 1

Relational Bible Study (Stories)

Designed around a guided questionnaire, the questions move across the Disclosure Scale from "no risk" questions about people in the Bible story to "high risk" questions about your own life and how you would react in that situation. "If you had been in the story ..." or "the person in the story like me is ... ." The questions are open-ended—with multiple-choice options and no right or wrong answers. A person with no background knowledge of the Bible may actually have the advantage because the questions are based on first impressions.

The STORY   GUIDED QUESTIONNAIRE   My STORY
in Scripture   1 2 3 4 5 6 7 8   compared

TRACK 1: Light RELATIONAL BIBLE STUDY	TRACK 2: Heavy INDUCTIVE BIBLE STUDY
• Based on Bible stories • Open-ended questions • To share your spiritual story	• Based on Bible teachings • With observation questions • To dig into Scripture

---

Track 2

Inductive Bible Study (Teachings)

For groups who know each other, TRACK 2 gives you the option to go deeper in Bible Study, with questions about the text on three levels:

- • Observation: What is the text saying?
- • Interpretation: What does it mean?
- • Application: What are you going to do about it?

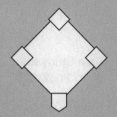

Group Building

The Baseball Diamond illustrates the four-step sharing process in bonding to become a group: (1) input; (2) feedback; (3) deeper input; and (4) deeper feedback. This process is carefully structured into the seven sessions of this course, as follows:

 Sharing My Story. My religious background. My early years and where I am right now in my spiritual journey.

 Affirming Each Other's Story. "Thank you for sharing ..." "Your story became a gift to me ..." "Your story helps me to understand where you are coming from ..."

 Sharing My Needs. "This is where I'm struggling and hurting. This is where I need to go—what I need to do."

 Caring for One Another. "How can we help you in prayer this week?" Ministry occurs as the group members serve one another through the Holy Spirit.

Mission / Multiplication

To prove that your group is "Mission-Driven," now is the time to start praying for your new "baby"—a new group to be born in the future. This is the MISSION of your group.

The birthing process begins by growing your group to about 10 or 12 people. Here are three suggestions to help your group stay focused on your Mission:

1. **Empty Chair.** Pull up an empty chair at the Caring Time and ask God to fill this chair at the next meeting.

2. **Refrigerator List.** Jot down the names of people you are going to invite and put this list on the refrigerator.

3. **New Member Home.** Move to the home of the newest member—where their friends will feel comfortable when they come to the group. On the next page, some of your questions about bringing new people into your group are answered.

Q&A

What if a new person joins the group in the third or fourth session?

Call the "Option Play" and go back to an EASY Bible Study that allows this person to "share their story" and get to know the people in the group.

What do you do when the group gets too large for sharing?

Take advantage of the three-part agenda and subdivide into groups of four for the Bible Study time. Count off around the group: "one, two, one, two"—and have the "ones" move quickly to another room for sharing.

What is the long-term expectation of the group for mission?

To grow the size of the group and eventually start a new group after one or two years.

What do you do when the group does not want to multiply?

This is the reason why this MISSION needs to be discussed at the beginning of a group—not at the end. If the group is committed to this MISSION at the outset, and works on this mission in stage one, they will be ready for multiplication at the end of the final stage.

What are the principles behind the Serendipity approach to Bible Study for a beginner group?

1. *Level the Playing Field.* Start the sharing with things that are easy to talk about and where everyone is equal—things that are instantly recallable—light, mischieviously revealing and childlike. Meet at the human side before moving into spiritual things.

2. *Share Your Spiritual Story.* Group Building, especially for new groups, is essential. It is crucial for Bible Study in beginner groups to help the group become a community by giving everyone the opportunity to share their spiritual history.

3. *Open Questions / Right Brain.* Open-ended questions are better than closed questions. Open questions allow for options, observations and a variety of opinions in which no one is right or wrong. Similarly, "right-brained" questions are

better than "left-brained" questions. Right-brained questions seek out your first impressions, tone, motives and subjective feelings about the text. Right-brained questions work well with narratives. Multiple-choice questionnaires encourage people who know very little about the Bible. Given a set of multiple-choice options, a new believer is not threatened, and a shy person is not intimidated. Everyone has something to contribute.

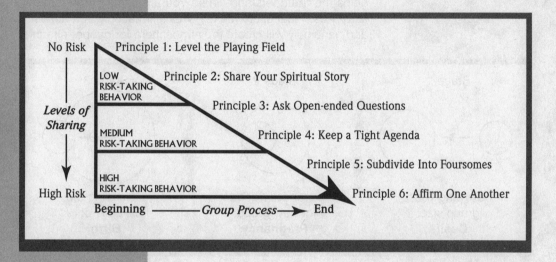

No Risk   Principle 1: Level the Playing Field

LOW RISK-TAKING BEHAVIOR   Principle 2: Share Your Spiritual Story

Levels of Sharing   Principle 3: Ask Open-ended Questions

MEDIUM RISK-TAKING BEHAVIOR   Principle 4: Keep a Tight Agenda

Principle 5: Subdivide Into Foursomes

HIGH RISK-TAKING BEHAVIOR

High Risk   Principle 6: Affirm One Another

Beginning ——— *Group Process*→ End

4. **Tight Agenda.** A tight agenda is better than a loose agenda for beginning small groups. Those people who might be nervous about "sharing" will find comfort knowing that the meeting agenda has been carefully organized. The more structure the first few meetings have the better, especially for a new group. Some people are afraid that a structured agenda will limit discussion. In fact, the opposite is true. The Serendipity agenda is designed to keep the discussion focused on what's important and to bring out genuine feelings, issues, and areas of need. If the goal is to move the group toward deeper relationships and a deeper experience of God, then a structured agenda is the best way to achieve that goal.

5. **Fearless Foursomes.** Dividing your small group into foursomes during the Bible Study can be a good idea. In groups of four, everyone will have an opportunity to participate and you can finish the Bible Study in 30 minutes. In groups of eight or more, the Bible Study will need to be longer and you will take away from the Caring Time.

Also, by subdividing into groups of four for the Bible Study time, you give others a chance to develop their skills at leading a group—in preparation for the day when you develop a small cell to eventually move out and birth a new group.

6. *Affirm the person and their story.* Give positive feedback to group members: "Thank you for sharing ... your story really helps me to understand where you are coming from ... your story was a real gift to me ... " This affirmation given honestly and genuinely will create the atmosphere for deeper sharing.

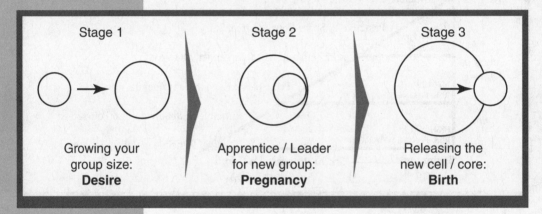

Stage 1	Stage 2	Stage 3
Growing your group size: **Desire**	Apprentice / Leader for new group: **Pregnancy**	Releasing the new cell / core: **Birth**

What is the next stage of our group all about?

In the next stage, the 201 BIBLE STUDY is deeper, GROUP BUILDING focuses on developing your gifts, and in the MISSION you will identify an Apprentice / Leader and two others within your group who will eventually become the leadership core of a new group down the road a bit.

what was good, so that through the commandment sin might become utterly sinful.

[14]We know that the law is spiritual; but I am unspiritual, sold as a slave to sin. [15]I do not understand what I do. For what I want to do I do not do, but what I hate I do. [16]And if I do what I do not want to do, I agree that the law is good. [17]As it is, it is no longer I myself who do it, but it is sin living in me. [18]I know that nothing good lives in me, that is, in my sinful nature. For I have the desire to do what is good, but I cannot carry it out. [19]For what I do is not the good I want to do; no, the evil I do not want to do—this I keep on doing. [20]Now if I do what I do not want to do, it is no longer I who do it, but it is sin living in me that does it.

[21]So I find this law at work: When I want to do good, evil is right there with me. [22]For in my inner being I delight in God's law; [23]but I see another law at work in the members of my body, waging war against the law of my mind and making me a prisoner of the law of sin at work within my members. [24]What a wretched man I am! Who will rescue me from this body of death? [25]Thanks be to God—through Jesus Christ our Lord!

So then, I myself in my mind am a slave to God's law, but in the sinful nature a slave to the law of sin.

1. What New Year's resolution or other commitment have you started with good intentions only to have it fizzle out?

2. What is the battle described in this passage?

3. Does Paul see the Old Testament Law as good or bad? In a nutshell, what does he say is its function?

4. In these verses, do you think Paul is talking about his life only before he became a Christian or about his life afterward also?

5. In what ways are Paul's struggles with wanting to do one thing but doing another common to us all?

6. Do you think Paul was a failure because of his struggles? Why or why not?

7. Do you ever feel like a failure because of your struggles? If so, how do you handle that?

8. How is Paul (and all of us) rescued from this struggle with sin?

❤ Caring Time / 15–45 Minutes

LEADER:
Ask the group, "Who are you going to invite next week?"

During your time of prayer, remember the people who shared and what they said. If you don't know how to begin, finish this sentence:

"Lord, I want to talk with you about my friend ..."

Don't forget to keep praying for the empty chair and inviting people to your group.

Reference Notes

Summary. In 7:5 Paul could be understood to be saying that the Old Testament Law brought to humanity both sin and death. Through two questions put in the mouth of his hypothetical opponent (vv. 7,13) he lays to rest these charges. In verses 7–12 he shows that the Law is not evil (sinful) and in verse 13 he shows that the Law is not that which brings death. Paul then continues in an autobiographical vein in verses 14–25.

7:7 *Is the law sin?* It might seem that this is what Paul is saying in passages such as Romans 5:20; 6:14 and 7:1–6. In fact, in verse 7 he shows that far from being evil or sinful, the Law serves first to reveal sin. It is like a finger pointing, "see that over there, that is what sin is."

I. In Greek, "ego." Throughout the remainder of chapter 7, Paul uses the first person singular (I, me) raising the question of who exactly he is referring to. In verses 7–13, he is probably using the first person singular in the sense of thinking of himself as a representative of humanity in general. He is not doing this merely for rhetorical reasons but also because it reflects his own pre-Christian experience.

7:8 *opportunity.* This word is used to describe a military base, which provides the starting point or bridgehead from which an active assault is launched.

produced in me. The Law provokes sin (its second function), not simply by pointing out forbidden fruit, but by being misunderstood as setting an unreasonable limitation on one's personal freedom (thus inducing resentment and rebellion).

sin. Here personified as a vital power with an evil intention.

dead. Sin is dead in the sense of being "inactive" until a prohibition comes along and rouses it to defiance.

7:9–11 Throughout this passage, Paul probably has in mind Genesis 3. The command in Genesis 2:17 not to eat from the tree of the knowledge of good and evil was given with the good of humanity in mind, but the serpent twisted the benevolent prohibition into a deadly temptation. This is an illustration of verse 8: prohibition produced covetous desire.

7:9 *alive apart from law.* Paul may be thinking autobiographically when, as a Jewish child prior to his bar mitzvah at age 13, he had no obligation to the Law; or he may be thinking in a more general sense of the period between Adam and Moses (see Rom. 5:13–14).

I died. Though living physically after the Law came, he fell under its judgment (i.e., under the sentence of death). This is the third function of the Law: it identifies the penalty for sin.

7:12 *holy.* At its root the word means "different" (i.e., of another realm of existence). The Law is divine in origin and authority. It is God's voice.

7:14–25 In this section (as in verses 7–13), the problem is not with the Law but with the sin that dwells within. The Law is good. People want to follow it, but find they cannot—at least not in their own strength. And so tension results. Paul illustrates this conflict vividly out of his own pre-Christian experience. As a sincere and dedicated Pharisee truly seeking God's way, he finds that despite his love of the Law and desire to do good, he simply cannot escape the domination of sin. (It must be noted that while this interpretation of the passage is favored by people like Origen, Wesley, and Dodd, still others like Calvin, Luther, and Barth feel that Paul is talking about his experience as a Christian. They argue that only a mature Christian has a sober enough view of himself to utter the cries of despair in vv. 18 and 24, while simultaneously delighting in God's Law as in v. 22).

7:14 The contrast is between the Law (which reflects God's mind) and unaided human nature (which is enemy-occupied territory).

the law is spiritual. It comes from God and therefore bears his divine authority (see Acts 1:16). It is important for Paul to say this lest his first-century Jewish audience misunderstand him to be departing from the Old Testament.

unspiritual. Literally, "composed of flesh," mere "flesh and blood," of flesh and not of spirit.

7:17 Not an excuse but a confession—"I want to do good but can't." The problem is not with the Law, but with sin.

7:18 *my sinful nature.* Literally, "flesh." The idea is not that one part of a person is "sinful" while another part is "spiritual." Rather, this is the whole person seen from one point of view; in this case, in terms of unaided human nature. "Now human nature or 'flesh,' it cannot be overstressed, is not for Paul or in biblical thought, in itself evil. But it is weak and mortal—it is the antithesis of God who is 'spirit' and power" (Robinson). Note that the "desire to do good" is part of this "sinful nature."

7:14–20 "We may summarize the teaching of these two parallel sections thus: First comes our condition: I know myself to be indwelt by the flesh, which contains no good but (if I am left to myself) holds me captive. Next the resulting conflict: I cannot do what I want, but I do what I detest. Finally the conclusion: if my actions are thus against my will, the cause is sin which dwells within me. All along, what Paul is seeking to do is to expose the no-goodness of our flesh to convince us that only the Holy Spirit can deliver us" (Stott).

7:21 *this law.* Not the Old Testament Law, but the other law mentioned in verse 23. Here Paul stands back from the experience itself and defines the nature of the inner conflict in the theological terms.

7:22–23 The law of the mind resides in the inner being. It delights in God's law in contrast to the law of sin, which is at work in the members and wars against God's law.

7:23 *law of sin.* The power exercised over humans by sin.

7:24 The nearer people come to God, the more aware they are of how short they fall of perfection. This is the cry of anguish and despair of one who longs to be free from slavery to sin and domination by the Law.

7:25 Who indeed will rescue him? Why, it is none other than the Lord Jesus Christ who met Paul on the Damascus Road, through whose death he at last found the long sought after freedom from slavery to sin and bondage to the Law. Paul goes on in Romans 8 to describe the freedom from sin and death brought about by the Spirit.

COMMENT There is an inner principle in all peple that inclines them to failure. Failure is normal; success is the surprise. Here Paul identifies the reason for this: It is sin dwelling in us. And the word sin in the New Testament refers not just to active transgression but also to falling short of what should be (i.e., failure). But Paul does not end with this fact. He goes on in Romans 8 to describe the freedom from sin and death brought about by the Spirit.

SESSION

5

Stress From Conflict

3-PART AGENDA

ICE-BREAKER
15 Minutes

BIBLE STUDY
30 Minutes

CARING TIME
15–45 Minutes

Life would be so much easier without conflict. Nations war with nations, and people die and are maimed. Conflict in the workplace creates ulcers and unemployment. Interpersonal conflict can end friendships and marriages. Conflict between parents and children can create runaways and sleepless nights.

Conflict hurts. Conflict undermines our whole world. Conflict dulls our life. Conflict brings physical disorders, psychological stress, emotional anguish and behavioral problems. In other words, conflict brings great stress. We must deal with conflict if we are to be healthy people.

> **LEADER: If you haven't already, now is the time to start thinking about the next step for your group. Take a look at the 201 courses (the second stage in the small group life cycle) on the inside of the back cover.**

In the following studies, first we see Jesus dealing with conflict (he is at odds with the religious authorities) and then we see Paul instructing the Christians at Rome about how to deal with relationships of conflict. Their examples and the principles they demonstrate give us valuable insights into how we can cope with our own conflicts.

Ice-Breaker / 15 Minutes

Things That Drive You Crazy. Here's a list of things that drive a lot of people crazy. Do they drive you crazy, too? As someone reads through the list that appears on the next page, share your responses to each situation.

	YES	NO	SOMETIMES
bathtub rings that aren't yours	❏	❏	❏
waiting at stoplights	❏	❏	❏
people who constantly channel-surf	❏	❏	❏
dripping faucet	❏	❏	❏
someone talking during a movie	❏	❏	❏
losing one sock	❏	❏	❏
not enough toilet paper	❏	❏	❏
someone who is always late	❏	❏	❏
someone who sings in the car	❏	❏	❏
boring speakers or teachers	❏	❏	❏
a motormouth	❏	❏	❏
preempting of a television program	❏	❏	❏
getting cut off in traffic	❏	❏	❏
getting put on hold on the phone	❏	❏	❏
people who take up two parking spaces	❏	❏	❏
an itch you can't reach	❏	❏	❏
screeching chalk on a chalkboard	❏	❏	❏
annoying song that gets stuck in your head	❏	❏	❏
people who crack their knuckles	❏	❏	❏
people who crack their gum	❏	❏	❏
people who chew with their mouths open	❏	❏	❏
backseat drivers	❏	❏	❏
telephone solicitors	❏	❏	❏
someone leaving the toilet seat up	❏	❏	❏

Bible Study / 30 Minutes

Option 1 / Gospel Study

Mark 11:15–19 / Conflict Resolution

Read Mark 11:15–19 and discuss your responses to the following questions with your group. As the passage begins, Jesus arrives at the temple in Jerusalem and discovers that the religious establishment has set up tables and is overcharging the people.

15On reaching Jerusalem, Jesus entered the temple area and began driving out those who were buying and selling there. He overturned the tables of the money changers and the benches of those selling doves, 16and would not allow anyone to carry merchandise through the temple courts. 17And as he taught them, he said, "Is it not written:

" 'My house will be called
a house of prayer for all nations'?

But you have made it 'a den of robbers.' "
18The chief priests and the teachers of the law heard this and began looking for a way to kill him, for they feared him, because the whole crowd was amazed at his teaching.
19When evening came, they went out of the city.

COMMENT

Things were not what they should be in the temple. This was meant to be the place where God was honored and worshiped. And yet the outer court (which was the only place pious Gentiles could worship) had been turned into a raucous oriental bazaar. Doves (which were the only sacrifice the poor could afford) cost 20 times more than the ones purchased from outside vendors. The money changers who exchanged the various coins of the Roman Empire into shekels—the only currency acceptable to pay the temple tax—charged the equivalent of one-half day's wage for this simple act. What conflict this must have caused the people! They were being taken advantage of, and yet they had no choice if they were to fulfill their religious obligations. Jesus openly and directly confronts these injustices.

1. Who does Jesus resemble in this story?
❐ a bouncer   ❐ a fiery prophet
❐ a Marine sergeant   ❐ a political activist
❐ a bull in a china shop

"All men have in them an instinct for conflict, at least all healthy men."
—Hilaire Belloc

2. Are you a little surprised to see Jesus in this passage turning over tables and driving money changers out of the temple?
❐ Yes—I always thought Jesus was a man of peace.
❐ Yes—I have been taught "peace at any price."
❐ Yes—maybe he could have been a little more diplomatic.
❐ No—I'm glad to see this story in the Bible.
❐ No—I know exactly how he felt.

3. When your parents had conflict, what were they more likely to do?
❐ yell and throw things   ❐ hit and fight
❐ not speak for days   ❐ talk it over
❐ talk sweetly between gritted teeth   ❐ other: _____
❐ I don't remember any conflict.

4. When in your life, and with whom, have you had your greatest interpersonal conflict?

☐ during childhood ☐ with parents
☐ during adolescence ☐ with brother / sister
☐ during young adulthood ☐ with spouse
☐ during middle adulthood ☐ with in-laws
☐ during late adulthood ☐ with children
☐ with self ☐ with teacher / coach
☐ with boss ☐ with coworker(s)
☐ with God ☐ with friend(s)

5. How do you handle interpersonal conflict?

☐ I let the pressure build up.
☐ I ignore all conflict until I explode.
☐ I pray for God's intervention.
☐ I immediately confront and resolve the problems.
☐ I involve a third person in conflict resolution.
☐ I absorb the stress from conflict.
☐ other:_____

6. What have you found helpful in dealing with the stress of anger?

☐ going for a walk or drive ☐ talking to God about it
☐ talking to someone about it ☐ writing out my feelings
☐ doing some physical exercise ☐ other:_____
☐ confronting the situation

Option 2 / Epistle Study

Romans 12:9–21 / Loving Relationships

In this section of Paul's letter to the Romans, he describes relationships between Christians. In verses 14–21, he will conclude this section by discussing the question of how to relate to those who aren't Christians. Read Romans 12:9–21 and discuss your responses to the following questions with your group.

⁹Love must be sincere. Hate what is evil; cling to what is good. ¹⁰Be devoted to one another in brotherly love. Honor one another above yourselves. ¹¹Never be lacking in zeal, but keep your spiritual fervor, serving the Lord. ¹²Be joyful in hope, patient in affliction, faithful in prayer. ¹³Share with God's people who are in need. Practice hospitality.

¹⁴Bless those who persecute you; bless and do not curse. ¹⁵Rejoice with those who rejoice; mourn with those who mourn. ¹⁶Live in harmony with one another. Do not be proud, but be willing to associate with people of low position. Do not be conceited.

¹⁷Do not repay anyone evil for evil. Be careful to do what is right in the eyes of everybody. ¹⁸If it is possible, as far as it depends on you, live at peace with everyone. ¹⁹Do not take revenge, my friends, but leave room for God's wrath, for it is written: "It is mine to avenge; I will repay," says the Lord. ²⁰On the contrary:

> *"If your enemy is hungry, feed him;*
> *if he is thirsty, give him something to drink.*
> *In doing this, you will heap burning coals on his head."*

²¹Do not be overcome by evil, but overcome evil with good.

1. On a scale of 1 ("peace at any price") to 10 ("let's have it out"), how would you rate yourself on dealing with conflict?

2. Looking over this passage as a whole, how would you define what "love" is all about?

3. Which of Paul's admonitions do you have the most difficulty with?
   ❏ "honor one another above yourselves"
   ❏ "share with God's people who are in need"
   ❏ "bless those who persecute you"
   ❏ "rejoice with those who rejoice; mourn with those who mourn"
   ❏ "be willing to associate with people of low position"
   ❏ "live at peace with everyone"
   ❏ "do not take revenge"

4. Based on verses 9–13, rate your small group's experience by using the inventory below:

   LOVE TEST: We can be totally honest and open with each other in a spirit of love.

   GOODNESS TEST: We can share our struggles to be "God's people" with one another without fear or embarrassment.

   BROTHERLY LOVE TEST: We have a bond of love for each other like a family.

   HONOR TEST: We build up one another and consider each other's interests above our own.

   ZEAL TEST: We encourage one another to keep spiritually alive— red-hot in our spiritual faith.

41

JOY, PATIENCE AND FAITHFULNESS TEST: We are committed to support each other through personal trials, tribulations and hardships.

HOSPITALITY TEST: We are open to being a hostel—not only for each other, but also for hurting people who need a place to stay or belong.

5. In concluding these tests, what letter grade would you give your group so far for the goal of getting acquainted with each other—beyond a surface level? What grade would you give your group so far for the goal of growing numerically?

6. Who do you have the greatest difficulty living at peace with at this time in your life? What can you do this week, in a practical way, to live at peace with that person?

 # Caring Time / 15–45 Minutes

Take time at the close to share any personal prayer requests. Answer the question:

"How can we help you in prayer this week?"

LEADER: Ask the group, "Who are you going to invite next week?"

Then go around and let each person pray for the person on their right. Finish the sentence,

*"Our Father, I want to speak to you about
my friend _____."*

As you close, include a prayer for the bonding of your group members, as well as for the numerical growth of the group.

Reference Notes

Summary. Paul now offers a series of loosely connected exhortations by way of further explanation of Romans 12:1–2, focused first on relationships between Christians (vv. 9–13) and then on relationships with those outside the church (vv. 14–21).

12:9 *Love.* *Agape*, self-giving action on behalf of others made possible by God's Spirit. Thus far in Romans when Paul spoke of love, it was in reference to God's love (1:7; 5:5,8; 8:35,37,39; 9:13,25; 11:28). There is one exception to this, namely 8:28, where he speaks of a person's love for God. But here in 12:9 the focus shifts. Paul's concern is how the Christian relates to other people. This becomes especially clear in 13:8–10. "God in his love has claimed us wholly for Himself and for our neighbors, and the love, of which Paul speaks here, is the believer's 'yes,' in thought and feeling, word and deed, unconditional and without reservation, to that total claim of the loving God, insofar as it relates to the neighbor—a 'yes,' which is no human possibility but the gracious work of the Holy Spirit" (Cranfield).

sincere. Genuine, not counterfeit or showy. It is possible to pretend (even to one's self) to love others. John Calvin wrote: "It is difficult to express how ingenious almost all men are in counterfeiting a love which they do not really possess. They deceive not only others, but also themselves, while they persuade themselves that they have a true love for those whom they not only treat with neglect, but also in fact reject."

Hate / cling. Evil (a settled attitude of pursuing a way of life that runs counter to God's character) is to be avoided, while that which reflects God's nature is to be sought after and embraced.

12:10 *brotherly love.* A second word for love is used here, *philadelphia*, denoting the tender affection found in families, now said to be appropriate to those in the church—which is the Christian's new family.

Honor. Since other Christians are in union with Christ, they are to be honored "above yourselves" because Christ is mysteriously present in them (Cranfield).

12:11 *fervor.* This Greek word is also used of water which is boiling (or of metal, like copper, which is glowing red-hot).

12:12 What makes it possible to endure affliction is a joyful hope in one's secure inheritance in the age to come, coupled with daily, continuous prayer.

12:13 In Romans 12:2, Paul had urged his readers: "Do not conform any longer to the pattern of this world, but be transformed by the renewing of your mind." To be "renewed" is not just an interior matter of mind and emotions, but involves concrete outer action such as giving to those in need.

12:14–21 The emphasis here is on the Christian's relationship to those outside the church.

12:14 "Not only to refrain from desiring that harm should come to those who are persecuting us, but to desire good to them and to show that this desire is no mere pretense by actually praying for God's blessing upon them (it should be remembered that blessing and cursing are very serious matters in the New Testament as well as the Old Testament)—this is clearly opposed to what is natural to us" (Cranfield). A clear example of how "the renewing of our minds" is opposed to "the pattern of this world."

12:15 Believers demonstrate love to nonbelievers by being sensitive and responsive to their joys and sorrows.

12:16 Christians ought to provide a model of harmony for the world around them. Avoiding haughtiness, they ought to put in its place unselfconscious association with all types of people.

12:17a *Do not repay anyone evil for evil.* A common Christian teaching. See 1 Thessalonians 5:15 and 1 Peter 3:9.

12:17b Christians are called upon to do not just what the consensus calls "good," but those things that are inherently "good." These deeds will be recognized as such by those of good will.

12:18 *live at peace.* This is the prevailing principle in these verses. Christians are to work at creating harmonious relationships with all.

12:19–20 Seeking peace means doing away with the principle of revenge and the continual escalation of violence. Using quotes from Deuteronomy 32:35 and Proverbs 25:21–22, Paul reminds Christians that they are to leave judgment to God while they do all in their power to turn an enemy into a friend.

12:20 *burning coals.* Providing kindness of every sort to one's enemies may induce the kind of inner shame that leads to repentance, and hence to reconciliation and true friendship.

12:21 People who retaliate have allowed evil to overcome them. They have given in to their evil desires and have become like their enemy.

SESSION

6

Stress From Loss

3-PART AGENDA

ICE-BREAKER
15 Minutes

BIBLE STUDY
30 Minutes

CARING TIME
15–45 Minutes

It is nearly impossible to go through life without experiencing at least one major loss. Some people lose their health; others lose money and security; still others lose their freedom or self-respect. But perhaps the most painful loss of all is to lose a loved one—a child, a friend, a spouse or a parent. Loss can produce some of the most intense stress we may ever experience. In this session, we will deal with loss as a major contributor to stress.

> **LEADER: This is the next to last session in this course. At the end of the course, how would you like to celebrate your time together? With a dinner? With a party? With a commitment to continue as a group?**

In Option 1, we will see how the loss of hope affected two of Jesus' disciples. We will look at two people (in Luke's Gospel) who lost their faith after the Crucifixion. And for those doing the Option 2 Study, we will see the apostle Paul's reaction when he was not in control of his world. While a time of loss can be a stressful and painful experience, it can also bring a greater understanding of life.

Remember in this session the issue is your life. Use the Scripture passages to walk into your story with your group.

Ice-Breaker / 15 Minutes

Take a few moments to complete this do-it-yourself stress test. Circle the events you have experienced within the past year. Total your score. If it's more than 150 points, you're probably living under a lot of stress. (If you feel comfortable, share your score with the group.)

EVENT	STRESS POINTS
death of spouse	100
divorce	73
marital separation	65
jail term	63
death of family member	63
personal injury or illness	53
marriage	50
loss of job	47
retirement	47
marital reconciliation	45
health problem in family	44
pregnancy	40
sex difficulties	39
gain of new family member	39
business readjustment	39
change in financial state	38
death of close friend	37
change in line of work	36
arguments with spouse	35
large mortgage taken out	31
foreclosure on mortgage / loan	30
change in work responsibilities	29
son or daughter leaves home	29
trouble with in-laws	29
major personal achievement	28
spouse starts or stops work	26
change in living conditions or residence	25
revision of personal habits	24
trouble with boss	23
change in work hours	20
change in church involvement	20

TOTAL SCORE_____

Bible Study / 30 Minutes

Option 1 / Gospel Study

Luke 24:13–35 / Lost and Found

Read Luke 24:13–35 and discuss your responses to the following questions with your group. This passage takes on Easter Sunday, the day Jesus rose from the dead. The two disciples in this story are not two of the remaining 11 apostles, but two followers of Jesus who probably lived near Jerusalem and were returning home after Passover.

[13]Now that same day two of them [Jesus' disciples] were going to a village called Emmaus, about seven miles from Jerusalem. [14]They were talking with each other about everything that had happened. [15]As they talked and discussed these things with each other, Jesus himself came up and walked along with them; [16]but they were kept from recognizing him.

[17]He asked them, "What are you discussing together as you walk along?"

They stood still, their faces downcast. [18]One of them, named Cleopas, asked him, "Are you only a visitor to Jerusalem and do not know the things that have happened there in these days?"

[19]"What things?" he asked.

"About Jesus of Nazareth," they replied. "He was a prophet, powerful in word and deed before God and all the people. [20]The chief priests and our rulers handed him over to be sentenced to death, and they crucified him; [21]but we had hoped that he was the one who was going to redeem Israel. And what is more, it is the third day since all this took place. [22]In addition, some of our women amazed us. They went to the tomb early this morning [23]but didn't find his body. They came and told us that they had seen a vision of angels, who said he was alive. [24]Then some of our companions went to the tomb and found it just as the women had said, but him they did not see."

[25]He said to them, "How foolish you are, and how slow of heart to believe all that the prophets have spoken! [26]Did not the Christ have to suffer these things and then enter his glory?" [27]And beginning with Moses and all the Prophets, he explained to them what was said in all the Scriptures concerning himself.

[28]As they approached the village to which they were going, Jesus acted as if he were going farther. [29]But they urged him strongly, "Stay with us, for it is nearly evening; the day is almost over." So he went in to stay with them.

[30]When he was at the table with them, he took bread, gave thanks, broke it and began to give it to them. [31]Then their eyes were opened and they recognized him, and he disappeared from their sight. [32]They asked each other, "Were not our hearts burning within us while he talked with us on the road and opened the Scriptures to us?"

³³They got up and returned at once to Jerusalem. There they found the Eleven and those with them, assembled together ³⁴and saying, "It is true! The Lord has risen and has appeared to Simon." ³⁵Then the two told what had happened on the way, and how Jesus was recognized by them when he broke the bread.

1. Why didn't the two disciples in this story recognize Jesus when he joined them?
- ❏ They were preoccupied.
- ❏ They were depressed.
- ❏ They couldn't recognize Jesus in his resurrected body.
- ❏ They refused to believe their eyes.
- ❏ God kept them from recognizing him.

2. Do you think Jesus could have been a little more understanding with these two confused disciples?
- ❏ Well, he was a little harsh with them.
- ❏ No, I think they deserved it.
- ❏ He wasn't harsh—he was their counselor.
- ❏ other: _____

3. When do you think the healing started to take place in their lives?
- ❏ when they started to verbalize their disillusionment
- ❏ when Jesus explained the Scripture to them
- ❏ when their hearts started to "burn"
- ❏ when they went back to the fellowship in the Upper Room and shared their story

4. What is the most significant loss you have experienced in your life?

❏ loss of loved one	❏ loss of job
❏ loss of freedom	❏ loss of hope
❏ loss of money / security	❏ loss of friend(s)
❏ loss of faith	❏ loss of self-respect
❏ loss of home	❏ loss of marriage
❏ loss of health	❏ other: _____

5. What were your feelings about this loss? (Check two or three.)

❏ helplessness	❏ anxiety	❏ grief
❏ despair	❏ sadness	❏ worry
❏ loneliness	❏ shock	❏ depression
❏ bewilderment	❏ fear	❏ sorrow
❏ anger	❏ guilt	❏ confusion
❏ heartbreak	❏ anguish	❏ hopelessness

6. What helps you recognize Jesus alongside you when you are dealing with a loss?
❏ reading Scripture
❏ a fellowship of caring people
❏ time away to be with God
❏ talking out my pain with a trusted friend/counselor
❏ focusing on worship
❏ other:_____

7. If Jesus were to suddenly come alongside you today and walk for a few miles with you, what do you think he would talk about ... or let you talk about?
❏ some of the struggles I am going through right now
❏ my family situation
❏ my job
❏ He probably wouldn't say a word. He would just be there.
❏ I don't know. I really don't know.

8. How would you describe your "walk" with Christ right now?
❏ headed the wrong direction
❏ headed the right direction
❏ up and down

"Faith draws the poison from every grief, takes the sting from every loss, and quenches the fire of every pain; and only faith can do it."
—Josiah Gilbert Holland

COMMENT

Like these disciples, we also understand the experience of pinning our hopes on what we know is certain to take place in the future: a great job will materialize, a wonderful spouse will appear, our children will succeed. But it doesn't always happen that way. Someone else is offered the job; the person you love doesn't feel the same way about you; your child drops out of school and lives off others. What once seemed so bright is now dull and tarnished. The dreams die. Energy fades. Where once there was hope, now there is despair. Is there any way to recover hope?

In this story, the hope that was lost is that Jesus would redeem Israel; that he would fulfill all of God's promises to them; and that they would once again become a great people. All of this was shattered by a Roman cross. But something happens to the two travelers. They who were "downcast" now feel their "hearts burning" within them. Hope rises again.

What happened? What brought about the change? In this passage, first they articulated what their hopes had been. Second, they found the answer to their dashed hopes was there with them all along. They just did not see it yet. Third, their eyes were opened by Jesus. He gave them new hope.

49

There is insight for us here. It would be wrong to suggest that all loss is merely a matter of not knowing the facts (in this case, that Jesus had been resurrected), and that things will be all right when they are made known. It is true, however, that the shock of loss often paralyzes our vision so that we see only what we have lost, and not what we have. We need new eyes to see our loss in its full context. How does this new vision come? It comes from Jesus. He brings us words of wisdom and insight (through Scripture and his people). It is he who also gives us the gift of life. His resurrection life is our resurrection life. As we touch that Life, we recover our life.

Option 2 / Epistle Study

Romans 8:18–25,31–39 / Ultimate Hope

Read Romans 8:18–25,31–39 and share your responses to the following questions with your group. This is a passage of encouragement which Paul wrote to Christians in Rome.

[18]*I consider that our present sufferings are not worth comparing with the glory that will be revealed in us.* [19]*The creation waits in eager expectation for the sons of God to be revealed.* [20]*For the creation was subjected to frustration, not by its own choice, but by the will of the one who subjected it, in hope* [21]*that the creation itself will be liberated from its bondage to decay and brought into the glorious freedom of the children of God.*

[22]*We know that the whole creation has been groaning as in the pains of childbirth right up to the present time.* [23]*Not only so, but we ourselves, who have the firstfruits of the Spirit, groan inwardly as we wait eagerly for our adoption as sons, the redemption of our bodies.* [24]*For in this hope we were saved. But hope that is seen is no hope at all. Who hopes for what he already has?* [25]*But if we hope for what we do not yet have, we wait for it patiently. ...*

[31]*What, then, shall we say in response to this? If God is for us, who can be against us?* [32]*He who did not spare his own Son, but gave him up for us all—how will he not also, along with him, graciously give us all things?* [33]*Who will bring any charge against those whom God has chosen? It is God who justifies.* [34]*Who is he that condemns? Christ Jesus, who died—more than that, who was raised to life—is at the right hand of God and is also interceding for us.* [35]*Who shall separate us from the love of Christ? Shall trouble or hardship or persecution or famine or nakedness or danger or sword?* [36]*As it is written:*

"For your sake we face death all day long;
we are considered as sheep to be slaughtered."

³⁷ *No, in all these things we are more than conquerors through him who loved us.* **³⁸** *For I am convinced that neither death nor life, neither angels nor demons, neither the present nor the future, nor any powers,* **³⁹** *neither height nor depth, nor anything else in all creation, will be able to separate us from the love of God that is in Christ Jesus our Lord.*

1. At what age did you first experience the loss of someone or something important to you? What was that loss?

2. If you had been one of the small band of Christians in Rome and faced the possibility of losing your life, your job, your family and friends because of your commitment to Christ, what would be your response to these words from Paul?

"God will not look you over for medals, degrees, or diplomas, but for scars."
—Elbert Hubbard

3. What does Paul mean when he says that "our present sufferings are not worth comparing with the glory that will be revealed in us" (v. 18)?

4. What is the difference between the hope of a Christian and wishful thinking?

5. What is the closest you have come to feeling abandoned? How can this passage of Scripture, especially verses 35–39, help you in such a time?

6. In light of Paul's promise that we can be more than conquerors over the powers that threaten us with loss, how well are you living out that promise?

7. What needs to be the next step you take to conquer the stress you've felt due to loss?

Caring Time / 15–45 Minutes

Take time at the close to share any personal prayer requests. Answer the question:

"How can we help you in prayer this week?"

Then go around and let each person pray for the person on their right. Finish the sentence:

"Our Father, I want to speak to you about my friend _____."

Reference Notes

Summary. The transition in Paul's thought from the former section (Rom. 8:1–17) to this new section (Rom. 8:18–27) really occurs at verse 17. There his focus shifts from the fact that Christians are the children of God to the fact that Christians are the heirs of God. It is this idea of inheritance that leads to the theme of verses 18–27: the hope which people have who are indwelt by the Spirit of God. In 8:18–27, Paul first discusses what it is that is hoped for (vv. 18–19,21,23b). He then sets this hope of glory over against the pain of the present (vv. 20,22,23–25). He ends by pointing out that the Holy Spirit "groans" alongside those who groan (due to their suffering).

8:18 *I consider.* This could be translated: "I reckon." Paul has used this same Greek word in Romans 3:28 ("we maintain") and in Romans 6:11 ("count"). In each case, he means by it a firm conviction which can be worked out logically from the Gospel message.

sufferings / glory. Paul defines the basic contrast that will be the subject of verses 18–27. His point: one's future glory (inheritance) vastly outweighs one's present distress (sufferings).

present sufferings. The persecution that Christians will experience in the time between Jesus' first coming and his future return. These are real; not pleasant, but slight in comparison with the glory ahead.

8:19–21 The fate of humanity and the fate of the universe are intertwined. Just as through Adam's sin, creation also fell (Gen. 3:17); so too through the redemption of the sons of Adam creation will itself be restored (Rev. 22:3). In this section, Paul has in view the second coming of Christ, at which time all that Christians now experience partially will be theirs completely. See 1 Corinthians 15:51–52 and Philippians 3:20–21.

8:19 *eager expectation.* The image is of a person with excited anticipation scanning the horizon for the first sign of the coming dawn of glory. The only other occurrence of this word is in Philippians 1:20.

for the sons of God to be rewarded. Christians are indeed sons and daughters of God here and now in this life. What Paul refers to here is the fact that they are, as it were, incognito. It will only be at the Second Coming that it is revealed for all to see who are, in fact, the children of God.

8:20 *For.* Verses 20–21 will explain why the creation waits with such eagerness for this revealing.

the creation. The whole of the nonhuman world, both living and inanimate.

was subjected. The verb tense indicates a single past action (see Gen. 3:17–19).

frustration. The inability of creation to achieve the goal for which it was created—that of glorifying God—because the key actor in this drama of praise (humankind) has fallen. This word is also translated "vanity," which is used extensively in the book of Ecclesiastes.

in hope. There was divine judgment at the Fall, but this was not without hope. One day, it was said, the woman's offspring would crush the serpent's head (Gen. 3:15).

8:21 will be liberated. Creation will be freed from its frustrating bondage at the time of the Second Coming when the children of God are also freed from the last vestiges of sin.

bondage to decay. All of creation seems to be running down; deterioration and decomposition now characterize the created order.

8:22 pains of childbirth. Such pain is very real, very intense, but also temporary (and the necessary prelude to new life). The image is not of the annihilation of the present universe, but of the emergence of a transformed order (Rev. 21:1). Childbirth was a common Jewish metaphor for the suffering that would precede the coming of the new age (Isa. 26:17).

8:23 firstfruits. Generally this term refers to those early-developing pieces of fruit that were harvested and given to God, but here the idea is of a gift from God to people. The experience by the believer of the work of the Holy Spirit is a pledge that one day God will grant all that he has promised.

we ... groan inwardly. One groans not just because of persecution, but because one is not yet fully redeemed. Believers' bodies are still subject to weakness, pain, and death. The believer therefore longs for the suffering to end and for the redemption of the body to be complete (2 Cor. 4:7–18).

we wait eagerly. In one sense a Christian is already an adopted child of God, but in another sense he or she has yet to experience fully his or her inheritance.

8:24–25 Hope is connected with patient endurance as in Romans 5:2b–5.

8:31–35 In one of his most eloquent passages, Paul hurls a challenge out to all who would oppose believers: Absolutely nothing can separate Christians from God's love.

8:31 Paul does not ask, "Who is against us?" In response, many enemies could be named: hostile society, Satan, indwelling sin, death. Rather, he prefaces the question with an assertion that "God is for us" and then asks,

"Who can be against us?" Therefore, all potential enemies fade into insignificance.

8:32 Again Paul does not ask, "Will not God not give us all things?" A response to that question would probably be ambiguous were it not for his preface, where he indicates that God has already given the supreme gift—his Son who died on humanity's behalf.

8:33–34 Paul's next two questions are set in the context of a law court. Their point: there is no charge that can now be effectively leveled against Christians to bring about their condemnation since God is the Judge who had already justified them (and Jesus is their Advocate who pleads for them).

8:35 In response to his final unanswerable question, Paul names those enemies that might appear powerful enough to separate believers from God's love.

8:36 Such trials are not new for God's people, as seen in the quote from Psalm 44:22.

8:37 *more than conquerors.* Literally, hyper-conquerors or super-conquerors.

8:38 *death / life.* For Paul, to die was no longer a threat—it was to "be with Christ" (Phil. 1:21–23). Life is used here in the sense of trials, distractions, and enticements that could easily lead one away from God.

angels / demons. Continuing his pairing of opposites, Paul says that neither benevolent nor malevolent spiritual powers need be feared. At that time in history, the Jews had a highly developed view of angels, feeling that everything in the world had an angel—the wind, clouds, hail—and that these angels were jealous of humanity, and hence sought to disrupt God's interest in us (Barclay).

present / future. Neither this age nor the events in the future eschatological age are to be feared.

8:39 *height / depth.* These words were used in first-century astrology to signify spirits that ruled in the sky above or below the horizon. Or the ference could be to the influence of a star at the height or the depth of its zenith. It may mean simply, as one would put it today, that neither heaven nor hell can separate Christians from God's love.

P.S.
If the next session is your last session together, you may want to plan a party to celebrate your time together. Save a few minutes at the close of this session to make these plans.

SESSION
7

Stress From Overload

3-PART AGENDA

☕

ICE-BREAKER
15 Minutes

📖

BIBLE STUDY
30 Minutes

♥

CARING TIME
15–45 Minutes

Over the past several decades, the word "burnout" has come into common usage. Burnout is the state of physical, intellectual, emotional and spiritual exhaustion. In contemporary society, burnout has reached epidemic proportions. It is most evident in people in the helping professions—nurses, social workers, teachers, doctors and ministers. None of us is immune from the debilitating effects of burnout. Athletes and coaches burn out from the wear-and-tear of intense competition. Parents burn out from the pressures of providing for their families.

> **LEADER: Read the bottom part of page M8 in the center section concerning future mission possibilities for your group. Save plenty of time for the evaluation and future planning during the Caring Time. You will need to be prepared to lead this important discussion.**

In the Option 1 Study, we see Jesus on the verge of overload as he contemplates his impending suffering and death. We can learn much from the way he handles his distress. And in the Option 2 Study (from 2 Corinthians), Paul shows how the "God of all comfort" can help us to avoid overload.

Ice-Breaker / 15 Minutes

Academy Awards. You have had a chance to observe the gifts and talents of the members of your group. Now, you will have a chance to pass out some much deserved praise for the contribution that each member of the group has made to your life. Read out loud the first award. Then, let everyone nominate the person they feel is the most deserving for that award. Then, read the next award, etc. through the list. Have fun!

DEAR ABBY AWARD: The person who cared enough to listen.

BILL COSBY AWARD: The comedian in the group who helped us laugh and not take ourselves too seriously.

more ⟶

ROYAL GIRDLE AWARD: The supportive person who drew us together.

WINNIE THE POOH AWARD: The warm, caring person when someone needed a hug.

ROCK OF GIBRALTAR AWARD: The person who was strong in the tough times of our group.

OPRAH AWARD: The person who asked the fun questions that got us to talk.

TED KOPPEL AWARD: The person who asked the heavy questions that made us think.

NOBEL PEACE PRIZE: The person who harmonized our differences of opinion without diminishing anyone.

PINK PANTHER AWARD: The detective who made us deal with Scripture.

CHARLES ATLAS TROPHY: The person who undergirded the group with their quiet, inner strength.

BIG MAC AWARD: The person who showed the biggest hunger for spiritual things.

FROG-PRINCE AWARD: The person who started out feeling low and ended up discovering great things.

Bible Study / 30 Minutes

Option 1 / Gospel Study

Matthew 26:36–46 / Wear and Tear

Read Matthew 26:36–46 and discuss your responses to the following questions with your group. This passage reflects Jesus' anguish over his imminent crucifixion. The heart of his prayer was for God's will to be accomplished, whatever the cost.

36Then Jesus went with his disciples to a place called Gethsemane, and he said to them, "Sit here while I go over there and pray." 37He took Peter and the two sons of Zebedee along with him, and he began to be sorrowful and troubled. 38Then he said to them, "My soul is overwhelmed with sorrow to the point of death. Stay here and keep watch with me."

39Going a little farther, he fell with his face to the ground and prayed, "My

Father, if it is possible, may this cup be taken from me. Yet not as I will, but as you will."

⁴⁰Then he returned to his disciples and found them sleeping. "Could you men not keep watch with me for one hour?" he asked Peter. ⁴¹"Watch and pray so that you will not fall into temptation. The spirit is willing, but the body is weak."

⁴²He went away a second time and prayed, "My Father, if it is not possible for this cup to be taken away unless I drink it, may your will be done."

⁴³When he came back, he again found them sleeping, because their eyes were heavy. ⁴⁴So he left them and went away once more and prayed the third time, saying the same thing.

⁴⁵Then he returned to the disciples and said to them, "Are you still sleeping and resting? Look, the hour is near, and the Son of Man is betrayed into the hands of sinners. ⁴⁶Rise, let us go! Here comes my betrayer!"

1. Why do you think Jesus went to Gethsemane to pray?
   ❏ It was part of his routine.
   ❏ He was stressed out and knew he needed strength and guidance.
   ❏ He wanted to provide a good example for his disciples.
   ❏ It was his last chance to ask God for a plan other than the cross.

2. Why did Jesus take Peter, James and John along with him?
   ❏ He wanted them on the lookout.
   ❏ He needed their support.
   ❏ He was testing their endurance.
   ❏ He wanted them to pray for him.
   ❏ He knew they needed to pray for themselves.

3. Where is the "Garden of Gethsemane" that you go to when you're feeling really overloaded?
   ❏ my bedroom   ❏ my favorite place outdoors
   ❏ church   ❏ the ballpark
   ❏ I don't really have a place.   ❏ other:_____

4. Which of these common symptoms of overload did Jesus exhibit?
   ❏ irritability   ❏ disappointment
   ❏ anxiety   ❏ annoyance
   ❏ depression   ❏ exhaustion
   ❏ fatigue   ❏ agitation
   ❏ sleeplessness

5. Are you exhibiting any of these common symptoms of overload?

6. When you were in high school, who did you turn to when you needed support in a tough situation? What qualities did this person have which made you turn to him or her?

7. When you face a time of stress overload now (as Jesus faced in Gethsemane), what do you look for most from your friends?

8. Of the following ways that Jesus coped with and overcame burnout, which ways would you find helpful?
   ❏ praying to his heavenly Father for strength and support
   ❏ appealing to his disciples (friends) for support
   ❏ accepting the reality of the situation
   ❏ acknowledging his feelings and moving ahead

Option 2 / Epistle Study

2 Corinthians 1:3–11 / Beating Overload

Read 2 Corinthians 1:3–11 and discuss your responses to the following questions with your group. The apostle Paul had to undergo great hardships to establish some churches. One of those churches was in Corinth. In this passage, he tells them about some of his experiences.

3Praise be to the God and Father of our Lord Jesus Christ, the Father of compassion and the God of all comfort, 4who comforts us in all our troubles, so that we can comfort those in any trouble with the comfort we ourselves have received from God. 5For just as the sufferings of Christ flow over into our lives, so also through Christ our comfort overflows. 6If we are distressed, it is for your comfort and salvation; if we are comforted, it is for your comfort, which produces in you patient endurance of the same sufferings we suffer. 7And our hope for you is firm, because we know that just as you share in our sufferings, so also you share in our comfort.

8We do not want you to be uninformed, brothers, about the hardships we suffered in the province of Asia. We were under great pressure, far beyond our ability to endure, so that we despaired even of life. 9Indeed, in our hearts we felt the sentence of death. But this happened that we might not rely on ourselves but on God, who raises the dead. 10He has delivered us from such a deadly peril, and he will deliver us. On him we have set our hope that he will continue to deliver us, 11as you help us by your prayers. Then many will give thanks on our behalf for the gracious favor granted us in answer to the prayers of many.

1. Which of your memories does this passage bring to mind?

2. Because God comforts us, what are we able to do for others?

3. What effect can stress or distress have in a Christian's life?

4. When experiencing distress and burnout, what can a Christian do?

5. What is the closest you have come to feeling like Paul did in verses 8 and 9?

6. Paul found that intense pressures led him to depend on God all the more. How do you respond to intense pressures? Do they deepen your walk with God or drive you away from God?

7. In what ways has suffering been a creative force for you?

COMMENT

Our tendency is to look at suffering as a sign of divine displeasure. In the early church, however, it was seen as the mark of the Christian. In the same way that our Lord suffered, so we too, as his people, may be called to suffer.

We are not to court suffering, nor is suffering good in itself. Suffering is not abnormal in this world, and God can use such suffering on our behalf. The implication is that suffering brings stress; but suffering (and stress) can be transcended, in part, by opening ourselves to the redemptive meaning of it.

Optional Self-Inventory. Often we do not recognize overload until we are too worn down to do much about it. The following exercise will help you determine if you are currently experiencing overload. (If you are comfortable, share the results with your group.)

Instructions: Indicate how frequently you experience each of the following statements. Use the scale below to rate each statement.

0 = almost never   2 = frequently
1 = infrequently   3 = almost always

_____ I am irritable with others (family, coworkers, etc.).

_____ I feel emotionally drained by my work.

_____ I have difficulty falling asleep at night.

_____ I lack motivation in my work.

_____ I am disillusioned with my work (including housework).

_____ I think, "Why don't people leave me alone?"

_____ I treat people more impersonally than I would like.

_____ I wake up tired and have difficulty facing another day.

_____ I consider myself a failure.

_____ I am bothered by stress-related ailments (such as indigestion, headaches, high blood pressure, etc.).

_____ I feel like I am at the end of my rope.

_____ I feel trapped in my work.

_____ I feel exhausted at the end of the workday.

_____ I feel people make a lot of demands on me.

_____ I feel unfulfilled and am dissatisfied with my life.

_____ TOTAL

Total your score. A score of 0–15 indicates that you are probably not experiencing overload. A score of 16–30 indicates that you are probably experiencing moderate overload (and should do something about it). A score of 31–45 indicates that you are probably experiencing severe overload (and definitely should do something about it).

Caring Time / 15–45 Minutes

1. Take some time to evaluate the life of your group by using the statements below. Read the first sentence out loud and ask everyone to explain where they would put a dot between the two extremes. When you are finished, go back and give your group an overall grade in the categories of Group Building, Bible Study and Mission.

GROUP BUILDING

On celebrating life and having fun together, we were more like a ...
wet blanket _____hot tub

On becoming a caring community, we were more like a ...
prickly porcupine _____cuddly teddy bear

BIBLE STUDY

On sharing our spiritual stories, we were more like a ...
shallow pond _____spring-fed lake

On digging into Scripture, we were more like a ...
slow-moving snail _____voracious anteater

MISSION

On inviting new people into our group, we were more like a ...
barbed-wire fence _____wide-open door

On stretching our vision for mission, we were more like an ...
ostrich _____eagle

2. What are some specific areas in which you have grown in this course about stess?
- ❒ seeing stress as a signal to take a serious look at my life
- ❒ learning to trust God with every area of my life—rather than to worry
- ❒ having a healthy, balanced attitude toward the meaning and demands of work
- ❒ accepting failure as part of life, and realizing that it can be an opportunity for growth
- ❒ accepting conflict as part of life, and understanding that I have a choice in how to respond to it
- ❒ accepting loss as a part of life, and appreciating God's gifts of hope and peace to survive loss

❏ taking advantage of the resources available to prevent or recover from overload or burnout

❏ other:_____

MAKE A COVENANT

A covenant is a promise made to each other in the presence of God. Its purpose is to indicate your intention to make yourselves available to one another for the fulfillment of the purposes you share in common. If your group is going to continue, in a spirit of prayer work your way through the following sentences, trying to reach an agreement on each statement pertaining to your ongoing life together. Write out your covenant like a contract, stating your purpose, goals and the ground rules for your group.

1. The purpose of our group will be ... (finish the sentence)

2. Our goals will be ...

3. We will meet for _____weeks, after which we will decide if we wish to continue as a group.

4. We will meet from _____ to _____ and we will strive to start on time and end on time.

5. We will meet at _____ (place) or we will rotate from house to house.

6. We will agree to the following ground rules for our group (check):

❏ PRIORITY: While you are in the course, you give the group meetings priority.

❏ PARTICIPATION: Everyone participates and no one dominates.

❏ RESPECT: Everyone is given the right to their own opinion, and all questions are encouraged and respected.

❏ CONFIDENTIALITY: Anything that is said in the meeting is never repeated outside the meeting.

❏ EMPTY CHAIR: The group stays open to new people at every meeting.

❏ SUPPORT: Permission is given to call upon each other in time of need at any time.

❏ ACCOUNTABILITY: We agree to let the members of the group hold us accountable to the commitments which each of us make in whatever loving ways we decide upon.

❏ MISSION: We will do everything in our power to start a new group.

Summary. As in other of his letters, Paul's greeting is followed by thanksgiving. Yet here there is a special intensity and depth to the praises he offers God for having recently rescued him at the last moment from death. This section is also part of Paul's defense of his own integrity (which he will focus on directly beginning in 2 Cor. 1:12). The Corinthians are preoccupied with his seeming fickleness (v. 17), but before they judge him they ought to remember his sufferings (vv. 8–9) from which they benefit (vv. 4–7).

1:3 The exact same phrase is used in Ephesians 1:3 and 1 Peter 1:3. This phrase had apparently become a common way of describing God (Father) and Jesus (Lord) as well as the relationship between the two (God is both God and Father to Jesus).

Praise. A word often used at the beginning of the Jewish prayers meaning "blessed is" or "blessed be." Paul is using a Jewish form for his prayer.

the God and Father of our Lord Jesus Christ. This puts a distinctively Christian twist on what was a common Jewish liturgical form of praise.

comfort. The most common word in verses 3–7, used 10 times in one form or another. Its root meaning is that of standing beside someone undergoing trial so as to encourage that person. It came to mean to encourage, to cheer, or to strengthen. One form of this word is used as a title for the Holy Spirit: the comforter (*Paraclete*). In the context of verses 3–11, "it is clear that comfort means not that Paul is consoled in his afflictions but that he is delivered out of them" (Barrett).

1:4 *our troubles.* This includes both the internal anguish and the physical hardships that Christians experience because of their choice to follow Jesus.

so that we can comfort. The purpose of the comfort God gives is to enable those so comforted to aid others who are being afflicted.

1:5 *the sufferings of Christ.* Paul probably means both the physical suffering by Christ and the suffering involved in bearing the sins of the world while on the cross.

our comfort overflows. In the same way that the suffering of Christ is redemptive and its benefits overflow to his children; so (in a lesser way) the suffering of his children overflow to others by way of the comfort they are able to offer the afflicted.

1:6 *comfort / sufferings.* In the apostles we see plainly the curious paradox of the Christian life—it involves both distress and comfort. The suffering here is not due to sin or disobedience; nor is it a sign of God's punishment. Suffering is part of the Christian experience, as it was of Paul's life (Acts 9:15–16) and the Lord's life.

patient endurance. This is not grim, bleak acceptance of difficulties, but active overcoming and victory in the midst of trial because of the confidence of the Lord's ultimate deliverance (see Col. 1:11).

the same sufferings. The nature of the suffering by the Corinthian Christians is not clear, though there must have been something happening; otherwise, the comparison loses its force.

1:8 *the hardships.* It is not clear to what hardships Paul is referring. It was probably not the riot at Ephesus, which Luke records (Acts 19:23–41), since Paul did not seem to be in any serious personal danger then. Perhaps Paul was acutely ill or faced physical violence of some sort.

Asia. The Roman province located on the western part of modern Turkey, of which Ephesus was a leading city.

under great pressure. "Burdened" or "weighed down" (the image is of an overloaded ship).

1:9 "Physical illness, the shadow of death, and the failure of his work in Corinth were among the causes that led to the breaking down of a man who, if any had ground for confidence in the flesh, he had more. The church at Corinth, like many since, thought it could bypass affliction on the way to comfort; the theme of this epistle is that this is impossible" (Barrett).

1:10 *He has delivered us.* Paul is content to be with the Lord if necessary (Phil. 1:21–24), but in the case he cites God did rescue him. The lesson Paul learned out of this is of great value both to him and to the Corinthians.

1:11 *prayers.* Paul points to the power of intercessory prayer.